UNIVERSITY OF NORTH CAROLINA
STUDIES IN THE ROMANCE LANGUAGES AND LITERATURES
Number 96

RACINE AND SENECA

RACINE AND SENECA

BY
RONALD W. TOBIN

CHAPEL HILL
THE UNIVERSITY OF NORTH CAROLINA PRESS

depósito legal: v. 960 - 1971

artes gráficas soler, s. a. - jávea, 28 - valencia (8) - 1971

TABLE OF CONTENTS

	Page
INTRODUCTION	11
PART ONE: SENECA	
Chapter I: Structure and Themes	17
Chapter II: Characters	29
PART TWO: THE SENECAN TRADITION IN FRENCH SIXTEENTH- AND SEVENTEENTH-CENTURY TRAGEDY	45
PART THREE: RACINE	
Chapter I: Themes: *La Thébaïde*	79
Chapter II: Characters: *Andromaque*	91
Chapter III: Structure: *Bajazet* and *Mithridate*	113
Chapter IV: *Phèdre*	130
CONCLUSION	151
SELECT BIBLIOGRAPHY	163
INDEX OF AUTHORS	171

Es incalculable la influencia de las tragedias de Séneca en la dramaturgia francesa clásica

José Ortega y Gasset, *Ideas Sobre La Novela.*

To my wife Ann

INTRODUCTION

Recent years have witnessed a growing fascination with the literary debt of the seventeenth century to the ancients, both Roman and Greek, and consequently a significant number of studies of influence have appeared. Racine has proved to be an especially fruitful source for this species of analysis. It is my intention to bring to light his considerable and important rapport with the Roman dramatist and philosopher Seneca.

The tragedies [1] of Seneca have caused, and continue to cause, great controversy as to their literary merits. Indeed it has been but recently that critics have thought it wise to reassess Seneca's value, and the result has been a remarkable rise in his fortunes. Nonetheless the hardened popular image of Seneca's plays as undramatic, uninteresting, and unworthy of imitation has survived, and it is due in great part to the tenacity of this view that the Senecan contribution to plays as great as Racine's has been widely minimized. Furthermore, the principal figure who has given impetus to ignoring his debt to Seneca is precisely Racine himself.

---

[1] There are ten tragedies in the Senecan corpus, nine of which are usually regarded as authentic: *Hercules Furens, Troades, Medea, Phaedra, Thyestes, Phoenissae, Oedipus, Agamemnon,* and *Hercules Oetaeus. Octavia,* though it appears under Seneca's name, is of doubtful authorship. Although it will be occasionally necessary to allude to the philosophical works authored by Seneca, I am basically interested only in his dramatic literature. For a review of the current scholarship devoted to Seneca the philosopher and to his role in the philosophical and religious formation of France's Renaissance, consult the masterful synthesis of le Père Julien-Eymard d'Angers: "Le Renouveau du Stoïcisme au XVIe et au XVIIe siècle," *Actes du VIIe Congrès de l'Association Guillaume Budé, 1963,* Paris, 1964, 122-153.

Though they have not furnished a systematic and detailed examination of Racine's relationship to Seneca, several scholars have investigated Seneca's role in certain Racinian tragedies. (See, for example, the works of Charles Dédéyan, Elliott Forsyth, R. C. Knight, John C. Lapp, Raymond Lebègue, and Jean Pommier, listed in my bibliography.) One of my goals has been to coordinate the findings of such separate studies, and to include them into the larger framework of my own research so as to create a picture of the significant literary affinity between Racine and Seneca without, however, wishing to belittle the contribution of other classical authors or of Racine's contemporaries and immediate predecessors.

The first of this book's three parts treats of Senecan dramaturgy. Pointing out the basic features of Seneca's theater will serve to dispel the notion that the plays are devoid of artistic technique and consequently lacking in interest. Seneca was interpreted in contrasting fashion by French and English dramatists. The English preferred to read the Latin plays as plays of horror and revenge, where infernal deities and excessive bloodshed were the rule. The French Renaissance tragedians, Racine's artistic forebears, looked to the other side of Seneca, where introspectio, guilt, and responsibility are enveloped in a style and tone suitable for lofty declamation. Since several Senecan elements, notably the elevated tone, were incorporated into the genre of tragedy by Racine's predecessors and thus became integral parts of the form Racine undertook to practice (and since no one, to my knowledge, has yet attempted to point out the French tragedies of the sixteenth and seventeenth centuries which are indebted to Seneca), I have included a second major division in my work, which concerns the "Senecan Tradition," and which will serve to show the ways in which Seneca exerted influence on serious drama from 1550 to 1660.

The line of influence from Seneca to Racine — that is, Racine's imitation and utilization of Seneca — is at times indirect (through the "Senecan tradition") but mainly direct. The traces of Seneca that are found in Racine reveal an intimate knowledge of the Roman dramatist in the original Latin. This is to be expected, of course, given Racine's classical training, particularly at institutions where men like the Jansenist master Lancelot were so preoccupied with things Latin.[2]

The final section of this work deals, then, with the affinity between Racine and Seneca as seen in the structure, characterization, thematic content, and style of Racinian tragedy. I must reiterate that the focus of this particular study remains on Racine, and it is in relation to him that Seneca will be considered. For my fundamental assumption is that Racine became one of the outstanding artists of western literature, not only because of his own innate talent, but also because he was, in his way, a "moderne" who had learned from the "anciens."

I wish to express my indebtedness to the late and regretted Professor E. B. O. Borgerhoff of the Department of Romance Languages and Literatures of Princeton University, who suggested this particular investigation, and to Professor Alfred Foulet, of the same department, for his helpful advice. I am also grateful to Professor Raymond Picard of the Sorbonne, whose views were invaluable in sharpening the original focus of this work.

Finally, I must acknowledge the very practical assistance of the General Research Fund of the University of Kansas, the Penrose Fund of the American Philosophical Society, and the Committee on Research of the University of California at Santa Barbara.

Professional journals have already published two fragments of this study: "Tragedy and Catastrophe in Seneca's Theatre" (*Classical Journal*, November, 1966); "Seneca in *Bajazet* and *Mithridate*" (*Studi Francesi*, May-August, 1969).

---

[2] Cf. his *Méthode pour apprendre facilement et en peu de temps la langue latine*, 1644.

PART ONE
SENECA

CHAPTER I

STRUCTURE AND THEMES

If we accept the trend of recent scholarship and acknowledge that Seneca's philosophy informed his drama,[1] we must also recognize that the best means to communicating a moral lesson would lie in creating a tragedy whose whole meaning, rather than just isolated maxims, would be didactic. We should not expect or want to distinguish between the moralist and the dramatist. And indeed Seneca's Stoic viewpoint does explain the frequent reappearance in his tragedies of several principal themes which are at one and the same time dramatically interesting and illustrative of Stoic moral philosophy.[2] However, an exploration of these themes should conveniently follow a discussion of the plots and structures which are their vehicle.

---

[1] For a listing of the works involved in this current movement, see Norman T. Pratt, "Major Systems of Figurative Language in Senecan Melodrama," *Transactions and Proceedings of the American Philological Association*, XCIV (1963), p. 199, n. 1.

[2] Seneca himself proclaims the didactic value of the theater in Letter 108 to Lucilius (L. Annaei Senecae, *Ad Lucilium Epistulae Morales*, ed. L. D. Reynolds, Oxford, 1965, II, 452): "Non vides quemadmodum theatra consonent quotiens aliqua dicta sunt qua publice adgnoscimus et consensu vera esse testamur?

                Desunt inopiae multa, avaritiae omnia.
                In nullum avarus bonus est, in se pessimus.

Ad hoc versus ille sordidissimus plaudit et vitiis suis fieri convicium gaudet...." "Have you not noticed how the theatre re-echoes whenever any words are spoken whose truth we appreciate generally and confirm unanimously?

The most profitable means to this end will be to select one drama, label it as "typical," for the sake of argument, discuss it in some detail, and then indicate what variations on this particular structure are to be discovered in the other plays. A comparison of this tragedy with its nominal Greek counterpart will further prove useful in demonstrating what Seneca has brought, in the way of originality, to a subject already celebrated by a Greek predecessor. This procedure will also be of subsequent assistance in distinguishing between the elements which Racine borrowed from Seneca, and those which he could have found in the Greeks. Accordingly, *Medea*, in both its Senecan and Euripidean versions, will be studied. Once such an investigation has been completed, we will be in a better position to define the general composite elements of a Senecan play.

Seneca's *Medea* opens with a monologue by the title-character (v. 1-55), in which she invokes the aid of the infernal gods in avenging herself against Creon, Creusa, and Jason. In her rage, she declares she has not yet conceived of punishments worthy of accomplishment by one who no longer has the innocence and naïveté of youth (49-50), "Haec virgo feci; gravior expurgat dolor: / maiora iam me scelera post partus decent," ["These things I did in girlhood. Let my grief rise to more deadly strength; greater crimes become me, now that I am a mother."] [3]

Thus the prologue sets the scene, identifies the principal characters, indicates Medea's mood, and creates a tense atmosphere by hinting strongly at the deaths of Creon, Creusa, and even the children. Though it is clear to Seneca's audience (quite familiar with the legend) what form her revenge would take, Medea herself has not yet determined to kill her sons.

A poor man lacks much; the greedy man lacks all.
A greedy man does good to none; he does
Most evil to himself.

At such verses as these, your meanest miser claps applause and rejoices to hear his own sins reviled."

[3] All references in the Latin text of Seneca are to the edition of Frederick Leo (*L. Annaei Senecae, Tragoediae*, Berlin, 1879). The English translations of the Senecan text are taken from *Seneca's Tragedies*, trans. Frank Justus Miller (London, 1927). I retain the punctuation changes of the Leo edition made by Miller, which bring the text into conformity with common English usage.

STRUCTURE AND THEMES   19

The ensuing choral ode is an epithalamium for Jason and Creusa. It recalls Medea to reality with a shock, and in the following episode she turns to the means of her vengeance. Despite the urgings of the nurse, she becomes enraged at Creon, determines upon Creusa as her victim, but pardons Jason as being merely a pawn. She blames her unfortunate love ("infelix amor") for her present condition, and again strikes the note of self-fulfillment heard in the first act (171):

> Nutrix: Medea.
> Medea: Fiam.
> [Nurse: "Medea."
> Medea: "Will I be."]

When Creon makes his appearance, she confesses her crimes, claiming they were committed for Jason. Her request to remain near her husband is denied, but Creon, begrudgingly and somewhat fearfully, does grant her one day to visit with her children before going into exile. Medea's reply heightens anticipation of the crime by its double entente (296-297), "Nimis est, recidas aliquid ex isto licet: / et ipsa propero," [" 'Tis more than enough, though thou retrench it somewhat. I also am in haste."]

The chorus then sings of Jason's conquest of the sea, and how this upset the plan of the universe. But what was the recompense for this victory? — Medea!

The third act finds the nurse describing Medea's fury, followed by the appearance of the heroine herself in a wild rage. The scope of her vengeance and the intensity of her criminal sentiments grow until, as a perfect Stoic example of passion's destructive effects, she looms as a powerful threat to the order of the entire universe (426-427): "Sola est quies, / mecum ruina cuncta si video obruta," ["The only calm for me — if with me I see the universe o'erwhelmed in ruins; . . ."]

At the height of her emotion Jason enters, seeking to excuse himself for his betrayal. He insists that he acted with the children's welfare in mind. The sight of him tones Medea's fury down to a bitter sarcasm and when Jason again counsels moderation for the children's sake, Medea perceives the weak point in his armor (549-550): "Sic natos amat? / bene est, tenetur, vulneri patuit locus," ["Thus does he love his sons? 'Tis well! I have him! The place to wound him is laid bare."]

Medea pretends repentance until Jason departs, then proceeds to the execution of her plans, which now concern not simply Creusa but also the children. She has the nurse prepare the fatal robe to be sent to her rival.

The chorus begins on the theme of "Hell hath no fury like a woman scorned," and passes on to a prayer for Jason's safety. We learn from this ode that the chorus is still ignorant of the true nature of Medea's designs.

The nurse's first words furnish a clue to the *raison d'être* of the fourth episode (670): "Pavet animus, horret...," ["My spirit quakes with horror...."] Instead of noting that Medea's incantations took place off stage during the choral ode, and then moving on to a new event (a tactic he had already employed for the marriage ceremony during the second choral interlude), Seneca chooses to lengthen the period of suspense and intensify the emotion of horror first aroused by Medea's decision to murder her own offspring. And indeed, Medea's magical ceremony is not only infernal but terrible and, at its peak, horrible. [4]

After the chorus describes Medea's savage demeanor and prays for her swift departure, a messenger dashes in to relate the deaths of Creusa and Creon, and to warn of the conflagration which threatens to consume the city. Medea appears and informs the nurse that flight is unthinkable until she has fully quenched her thirst for vengeance. However, she wavers between her deadly decision and a natural revulsion from such an act. Then, in her deranged state, she beholds an apparition of her brother, and to satisfy him, kills one child.

Medea remains in the grasp of a jealous rage, and because Jason was not a witness to her crimes, she minimizes their effect. When he comes upon the scene, she completes her revenge by

---

[4] In the brilliant "Introductory Essay on the Growth of the Senecan Tradition in Renaissance Tragedy" to *The Poetical Works of Sir William Alexander* (Manchester, 1921), editors L. S. Kastner and H. B. Charlton note (I, xxii): "Nominally Seneca's themes are the same as those of Greek drama; but the terror they there inspired was controlled by the religious awe which was at its basis; and that dissolved, they became in Seneca not terrible but horrible. It is precisely this horror which Seneca emphasizes."

slaying the second child, despite Jason's pleas, and throwing the body to him from the palace roof as she makes her escape on a dragon-drawn chariot. The drama ends with Jason's impotent curses following Medea into the clouds.

The better to appreciate Seneca's particular talent, let us now look at Euripides' *Medea*, which offers some striking contrasts with the Senecan story. For example, in the Greek play there is direct and rather ample exposition of material which the Latin dramatist will prefer to insert gradually, for the purpose of suspense, into the first two, even three episodes. Euripides has the nurse express a fear that Medea may take revenge on her children and her husband, because of her mad passion aggravated by Creon's decree of exile for her and the children.

While Medea's cries are intermittently heard, the chorus inquires as to the cause of such grief, for, in complete contrast to the Senecan conception, the chorus has a sympathetic interest in the principal figure. At the chorus's suggestion, the nurse induces her mistress to come out and talk to friends whose conversation may soothe her.

The justice of Medea's cause is explained in the second episode by the heroine herself. She is more helpless than the rest of her sex, for she is a foreigner. The chorus then promises to remain silent should Medea discover a means for punishing Jason, Creon, and the princess.

Creon appears and attempts to speed Medea on her way, but she feigns submission so well that he grants her one day's delay. After his exit, she announces her deception to the chorus, as well as her resolve to commit murder. Creon's fear of her magic powers has also suggested to her the very means: a lethal magic potion.

In the interlude the chorus continues to express sympathy for woman and for Medea in particular. In the following scene of confrontation, Euripides again touches on Jason's concern for his sons and on Medea's homelessness, thus foreshadowing the catastrophe and the denouement.

The chorus then prays for deliverance from excessive passion and jealousy, exile, and ingratitude. Though general in nature, the choral ode has an obvious and direct connection with preceding and succeeding matter.

Aegeus, in Corinth by accident, encounters Medea and swears to give her refuge in her helpless condition. Once he has left, she divulges full particulars concerning the poisoned gifts. Aegeus' unfortunate state of childlessness also suggests to her the most aptly cruel form of reprisal against her former husband. Norman T. Pratt demonstrates how these two points are intertwined: "Not only will Medea's children by their death create sorrow for Jason after he is made to think that he will retain them in his possession, but they will also be the means for the destruction of the princess by Medea's drugs and thus of the possibility of children being born from the new marriage. Viewed in this light the development of Medea's plans becomes one of the most subtle and effective examples of psychological motivation in Greek tragedy and it is not surprising that Euripides is its artificer." [5] Seneca disdains this subtlety since intense and powerful dramatic effects are his goals.

The chorus tries vainly to dissuade Medea from the dreadful deeds. The enchantress then deceives Jason into believing in her repentance by offering to send a wedding gift, borne by their children, to Glauce. In this scene, skillful use is made of dramatic irony and foreshadowing, sustained by the ensuing choral interlude.

After the messenger confirms the fact that the present has been delivered, Medea wavers concerning her children's fate, finally deciding upon the necessity of the crime.

The chorus leader's monologue on the advantages of childlessness is followed by the entrance of a messenger who informs the heroine of the deaths of Glauce and Creon, and she in turn rushes into the palace to put the final touch to her fiendish plan.

The last choral ode consists of a single strophe and antistrophe in which the chorus beseeches the gods to prevent Medea's insane act. The shrieks of the children are then heard while the chorus shouts to Medea to desist. When Jason is apprised of the deaths

---

[5] *Dramatic Suspense in Seneca and in his Greek Precursors* (Princeton: Princeton University Press, 1929), p. 78.

and is about to force his way into the house, Medea appears in her chariot to refute his charges with the statement that his ingratitude constituted the sole cause of the crimes. After a vicious argument, she disappears, bearing away the bodies of her dead sons.

The summaries of these two tragedies indicate the ways in which they differ structurally; and structural dissimilarities betray profoundly varying points of view. The Senecan play is more tightly knit precisely because it is completely "monocentric": it concerns the emotions, actions, and mental state of a single character. Whereas Euripides allows his secondary figures the opportunity to individualize themselves, Senecan minor figures are generally stiff or one-sided (e.g., Jason = Weakness) and act basically as confidants, as verbal instruments to engage in dialogue with Medea or to describe her activity. And so, even when she is not on stage, which is rarely (in two scenes out of twelve), Medea remains the topic and unchanging focus of the drama. Whereas Euripides seeks a range and profundity of emotional experience, Seneca prefers the powerful effect of a concentrated, almost obsessive approach.

The narrow focus of Seneca's attention can be appreciated by a comparison of the relative importance accorded to the fates of Creon, Creusa (Glauce), and the children. The active chorus in Euripides passes the last two-thirds of its time on stage in a state of concern for Glauce (third and fourth choral interlude), or for the children (monologue in the fifth episode, and fifth choral ode). In addition, Medea does manage to slay the children, but offstage.

Seneca portrays his chorus as concerned for Jason, but in an infinitely more general manner (cantica two and three). Like all Senecan choruses, it seldom intervenes in the action, except to pose questions or to come to the aid of a character. In fact, Pierre Grimal has observed that the role of the chorus in Senecan drama is essentially limited to the creation of "... une atmosphère, une sorte de décor spirituel au sein duquel vient se situer l'action ... le chœur devient tout naturellement l'orateur de la condition humaine, celle qui 'donne l'échelle' aux héros tragiques qui la dépassent, dans la vertu ou dans le crime."[6]

Once the chorus in *Medea* learns of the fatal gifts, its anguish redoubles, but it never approaches the state of *engagement* of Euripides' choral group, and thus Seneca's Medea is much more a solitary figure, the one who, cursed by fate and circumstances, brings evil into her relations with others. Moreover, the Senecan chorus never even suspects Medea's plans for her progeny, who are slain by her in full view of the audience. For these reasons, the spectator's interest is directed almost unfailingly toward Medea, and Seneca evidently planned his drama with this element uppermost in mind. Seneca's Stoicism supports this preference for penetrating and detailed analysis of the struggles between the rational and the irrational which take place within a Medea.

In *Medea*, as in his other plays, Seneca clearly seeks to portray the extremes of feeling. Even granting a remarkable degree of success in this respect to *Medea*, which develops an impression of growth in intensity and scope, one must admit that, in most of his other plays, Seneca fails to convey the desired emotional effect. One fundamental reason is that his style creates maximum intensity from the beginning, and one cannot proceed higher than the summit. To remedy this, the author multiplies his powerful rhetorical devices, but usually succeeds merely in dulling any effects that one or two well-wrought, incisive expressions could have gained.

The result of this rhetorically oriented style in *Medea*, as elsewhere, is that complete unity of tone exists, and further, that the language is of the most elevated and elegant kind. Indeed, the formal language attracts even more attention by the passionate outbursts expressed through it. (We shall see the importance of this aspect of Senecan tragedy when considering the Senecan tradition.)

The *Medea* accurately represents Seneca's approach to playwriting, and we may generalize on what we found in that play to describe the formal common denominators of Senecan tragedy.

---

[6] "Les Tragédies de Sénèque," *Les Tragédies de Sénèque et le Théâtre de la Renaissance* (Paris: Centre National de la Recherche Scientifique, 1964), pp. 4-5.

Any attempt at formulating a brief but inclusive definition of each of the five episodes is doomed to imprecision, if not error, because of the freedom with which the plays were composed. Nevertheless, there are certain discernible traits. The prologue [7] contains a dialogue (in three of the plays) or more likely a monologue (as in five plays) by a human or superhuman character, whose purpose is to identify and spark interest in the protagonists, to prepare the scene, to create anticipatory suspense through veiled reference to the outcome of the plot, and of even greater significance, to suggest the general nature of the moral situation which will develop.

In the second episode an important decision is made, setting the drama in action: for example, Medea's determination to revenge herself. Similar decisive action is taken by Atreus in *Thyestes*, Aegisthus and Clytemnestra in *Agamemnon*. *Hercules Furens* contains Lycus' determination to possess Megara or see her die, and in *Hercules Oetaeus* Dejanira resolves to enchant Hercules with a love potion. In the second division of *Oedipus* and *Phaedra* one can find a decision, but, contrary to what happens in the other plays, it does not constitute the indispensable event of the episode.

In the third division may be found a "return" scene, either (1) because the character who has come back is the bearer of significant news (Creon in *Oedipus*, Eurybateus in *Agamemnon*, the reappearance of Hyllus in *Hercules Oetaeus*), or (2) because his entrance, in itself, will have a forceful impact on the plot (*Thyestes, Hercules Furens,* Jason in *Medea,* Theseus in *Phaedra*). The appearance of the "returned" figure is absolutely essential to speeding the drama toward its climax, and this technique will be a very fertile source of *péripéties* in French classical drama, as, for example, in the reappearance of Thésée in *Phèdre*.

The fourth act very often contains a high point of the action. In this respect, *Medea* is an exception. In that play Seneca preferred to continue the foreboding atmosphere which would lend greater force to the climactic fifth episode. Moreover, the

---

[7] No attention will be given to the *Phoenissae*, because the text is of a fragmented nature.

unusually brief fourth division (eighty-five verses) of *Agamemnon* has as its only function the introduction of the title figure, and thus is different from *Hercules Furens,* in which the slaughter of Hercules' family furnishes a peak of action and of moral didacticism: Hercules' loss of reason causes destruction.

The denouements, finally, are varied and eventful. The Senecan repertory knows no calm endings, no gentle fading-away. The last act is that of the whole catastrophe in several plays or the final moment of it in those instances where it has been spread over two acts *(Troades, Thyestes).* In many instances this spectacle is related rather than presented on stage. The last act, furthermore, in almost all the plays contains the moment of tragic illumination.

And so, from the point of view of structure alone, Seneca does not merely follow the Greeks, but is an original dramatist. The fact that Seneca is thus worthy of imitation is a capital point to which I will refer when considering Racine's debt to him.

Now that the structural basis of Senecan drama has been established, we can profitably review the themes, and *Phaedra* will serve as a model for Seneca's thematic preoccupations, just as *Medea* revealed his structural organization.

An examination of the prologue of *Phaedra* uncovers once more the Senecan device of seeding those themes which will culminate in the events of the catastrophe. Phaedra bemoans her fate of being a foreigner, being married to an unfaithful husband, and being hounded by fears of the vengeance of Venus. This vengeance is hereditary, and stirs up in its victim the flames of an impure passion. When Phaedra announces her intention to die, the nurse offers to attempt to bend the inflexible Hippolytus, object of Phaedra's desire, but has no success with the young man who vaunts the benefits of the solitary, rustic life, far away from the corrupt city and the even more pernicious female sex.

In impatience heightened by unsatisfied sexual desire, Phaedra resolves to take matters into her own hands and attempts to ensnare Hippolytus in a political trap by offering him the throne. But she cannot contain herself, and gives full expression to her aroused passion, as does her French counterpart in Racine. Feeling tainted by this corruptive proposal, Hippolytus rushes off to the woods for purification. This "pollution" caused by the Latin

Phaedra is another element which will find its way, but with more sweeping effect, into Racine's *Phèdre*.

The sudden arrival of Theseus forces Phaedra into a choice between self-preservation by sinking lower into the mire of guilt and immorality, or certain disgrace, even death, if the truth be told. Under the nurse's guidance and urging, she chooses the former and deliberately lets Theseus entertain the implication of his son's guilt, which leads to the lethal curse upon the prince.

Like Euripides and Racine, Seneca employs the technique of a messenger to inform Theseus of Hippolytus' horrible death. The messenger explains that the prince's renowned beauty was fatal — a theme interlaced into the fabric of the plot in several instances. Since his paternal affection had not been entirely suppressed by Hippolytus' "crimes," Theseus is profoundly moved.

At this point Phaedra enters, sword in hand, to announce to all ("Audite, Athenae," v. 1190) that she cannot conceal the torment which has plagued her. Dying, she pronounces the word that characterizes the state of her soul: "impium" — guilty of a crime against the gods, (*Phaedra*, v. 1197: mucrone pectus impium justo patet ... ["my impious breast is bare to the sword of justice"]).

The hatred of Venus toward Phaedra's family operates as a hereditary curse to spark the illegitimate love whose close analysis forms the basis of *Phaedra*. We discover most of the major Senecan themes in this play: revenge, exile, suffering, politics, parental affection, taint and purification, suicide and death. But the focus is primarily on the effects of passion, heredity, and the injustice of fate's ways which, when intertwined, produce the tragic condition of the sensual but sensitive creature whose progressive mental and emotional states are under investigation by the dramatist. This subject, possessing as it does such inherent dramatic qualities, and permitting a soul-searching psychological analysis, naturally found its way into the Racinian repertory. Indeed, Racine was loath to eliminate from his *Phèdre* those events, those themes, even that focus which he encountered, certainly in French precursors, and as surely in the original source, Seneca.

The theme which has always been most closely associated with Seneca is, of course, revenge. In his works, the note of personal reprisal supersedes that of divine retribution found in the Greeks. As Kastner and Charlton have noted, "the Ghost is promoted from a supernumerary to a presiding position in the *dramatis personae*" [8] in Seneca. The Ghost lends a sense of religious duty to personal, especially blood revenge. Seneca has thus seized the dramatic possibilities of family strife, just as Racine will use the theme of "The Family in Disorder." [9]

If one examines the whole Senecan corpus from a thematic point of view, one perceives that, whether by a process of gradual illumination as in *Oedipus* and *Hercules Furens,* or by injecting a strong dosage of clear self-perception into his characters from the outset as in *Medea* and *Agamemnon,* Seneca wanted to emphasize the *conscience de soi* which is the fundamental characteristic of his creatures. In addition, he has placed them in situations where revenge, brought on by heredity, and fanned by envy, ambition, or fate, can only result in a vital, violent, dramatic clash where the most extreme of emotions are in play, irrevocably, and where the terrible awareness of self and of one's limitations may drive the individual to seek death as a final relief.

Evidently Seneca did not create entirely new themes, but his method of working old ones is noteworthy. He employed these subjects as a point of departure which permitted him to manifest his original talent.

A comprehension of Seneca's thematic material will be of assistance in an investigation of Racinian themes. But first a study of Senecan character, the dramatist's primary concern, is in order.

---

[8] *The Poetical Works of Sir William Alexander,* p. xxii.
[9] See John C. Lapp, *Aspects of Racinian Tragedy* (Toronto, 1955), p. 4.

CHAPTER II

CHARACTERS

In his *Poetics,* Aristotle acts as the "interpreter" for the Greek dramatists, and in so doing makes it clear that their preoccupation was the "imitation of an action," that is, the construction of a plot. Seneca's function, in literary history, was precisely to originate modern tragedy by diverting the center of attention from the plot and towards the study of the characters and their various mental and emotional states. The determination of the distinction between tragedy and catastrophe in each play of the Senecan repertory can be of significant assistance in appreciating Seneca's characterization. To this end I have elected to discuss those major figures who are important as typifying what is original in Seneca's tragic view, and who, at the same time, shed light on the unity (one might be tempted to say "single-mindedness") of Seneca's characterizations.[1]

Hercules

The character of Hercules furnishes an excellent point of departure, for he can be compared to himself, so to speak, by placing *Hercules Furens* beside *Hercules Oetaeus.* Secondly, this character is designed to inspire admiration more than pity or fear — a sentiment re-encountered as an essential ingredient in Corneille's theater and also in Racine's *Alexandre le Grand* and *Mithridate.*

---

[1] Léon Herrmann gives a much more detailed analysis of Seneca's characters on pp. 392-470 of *Le Théâtre de Sénèque* (Paris, 1924).

When first seen in *Hercules Furens*, the hero establishes himself and his principal traits in fifty lines: boastful, proud, cold to the point of ignoring his relatives in his haste to dispatch Lycus. The subsequent recounting of all his good works does not dispel the unsympathetic impression.

However, as the play progresses his particular nature reveals itself: inhumanly hard, fundamentally because he is more than human. The justice of his claims therefore awakens a feeling of admiration. But as Hercules is about to declare his conquest of all monsters, Juno has her revenge and he goes mad. He imagines the pathway to his deification impeded by Juno, and in his rageful attempt to clear away the obstruction, he slays his wife and sons. Seneca handles this scene deftly, and creates the impression that it was simply by goading Hercules' *amour-propre* and ambition to an extreme that Juno produced the fit of insanity. And so Hercules will be at least partly responsible for the murders, because of his self-esteem.

The colossal stature of the hero makes his fall all the more terrible, and the ensuing scene, wherein he gropingly learns the awful truth, arouses considerable sympathy, especially when the "inflexible" Hercules is reduced to crying out (1192), "Miserere, genitor, supplices tendo manus...," ["Have pity, father; see, I stretch out suppliant hands."]

The irony of the situaton is not lost upon the hero, for he sadly indicates that whereas his other feats were executed in accordance with Juno's commands, this deed originated in his will alone (1268), "laudanda feci iussus: hoc unum meum est," ["As for my glorious deeds, at others' hest I did them; this alone is mine."] It is interesting to see that even in his sorrow Hercules remains proud, refusing the slightest responsibility for one of his deeds to anyone but himself.

Human nature takes control, and Hercules sees no point to continuing his existence (1278-1282):

> Si vivo, feci scelera; si morior tuli.
> purgare terras propero — iamdudum mihi
> monstrum impium saevumque et immite ac ferum
> oberrat. agedum, dextra, conare aggredi
> ingens opus, labore bis seno amplius.

["If yet I live, I have committed wrong;
But if I die, then I have suffered it.
I haste to purge the earth of such as I.
Now long enough has there been hovering
Before my eyes that monstrous shape of sin,
So impious, savage, merciless, and wild.
Then come, my hand, attempt this mighty task
Far greater than the last."]

The struggle against this self-revulsion resolves itself, too quickly and therefore awkwardly, when Hercules submits to an Amphitryon who threatens suicide. Dramatically, the immediacy of Hercules' reaction appears to be a fault. Seneca does make his philosophical point, to be sure: Amphitryon's cry that his own death will have been caused by a Hercules returned to *reason* (whereas the massacre of the family was done by an *insane* Hercules) strikes terror into the heart of the stoic hero Hercules. Unwilling to offend against the dictates of reason, Hercules yields before Amphitryon's argument and consents to follow Theseus into exile at Athens.

The second Hercules proves to be more vain and aggressive than the first. In the *Hercules Oetaeus*, undoubtedly the poorest of Seneca's tragedies as well as the longest and most tedious (1996 verses against a mean of 1016 for the other plays), the principal figure takes command of center stage and never relinquishes it. His boastings, fierce claims to equality with the gods, and the recitations of his feats flow like a monologue, interrupted occasionally by the unimportant mutterings of a character or two. In again pursuing his goal of intense concentration, Seneca has strained to the breaking point the willing attention of the spectator.

This drama plays upon the same approximate theme as the other — namely, Hercules' struggle against an internal force which is undermining his spirit. Indeed, that part of the play which describes the torment due to Nessus' poison contains but one striking passage; it occurs precisely where Hercules' pride, courage, and self-composure desintegrate as he breaks into tears, exclaiming (1264), "O malum simile Herculi!" [O woe, invincible as Hercules!"]

However, his immediate recovery upon learning that it was fate, and not a human being that rendered him helpless, clarifies a major aspect of his character: the most severe of tortures for Hercules consisted not of physical torment, but rather of blows to his integrity and self-esteem. Once satisfied that he has not been defeated, he overcomes suffering and proceeds rapidly to the flames of the funeral pyre. The assumption that someone had laid him low was the cause of the hero's pain, because it posed the most serious threat to his reputation and conception of his own worth.

Hercules Oetaeus terminates with that event which has been prepared from the prologue: the apotheosis of the hero. Seneca evidently wishes to teach us that Hercules has passed from a state of passion to one of reason, and he therefore merits the highest rank among men: deified protector of the human race. This unusually non-tragic ending (the manner of death and the apotheosis are obviously to Hercules' great credit) stands alone in Senecan drama, but does fulfill the idea sown early in the play: Hercules' elevation to a place among the gods.

Hecuba and Andromacha

Hecuba and Andromacha resemble each other in that the seemingly impossible happens to them: their hopeless condition in the first act of the *Troades* grows, not better, but dishearteningly worse throughout, culminating in the lament-filled final episode. Each of these women grieves for a close relative. But Hecuba's torment proves more profound because of her consciousness of the role she has played — or that destiny has ordained that she play — in the destruction of the Trojan civilization. Indeed, the very first verses of the play sound the notes of Hecuba's conciousness of her association in Troy's fate (1-4):

> Quicumque regno fidit et magna potens
> dominatur aula nec leves metuit deos
> animumque rebus credulum laetis dedit,
> me videat et te, Troia: . . .

> ["Whoe'er in royal power has put his trust,
> And proudly lords it in his princely halls;
> Who fears no shifting of the winds of fate,

But fondly gives his soul to present joys:
Let him my lot and thine, O Troy, behold."]

Andromacha is a totally sympathetic character, a masterpiece of tenderness, devotion, and maternal love. Her drama consists in the choice that must be made between Andromacha-mother and Andromacha-wife (widow). In Act III of the *Troades*, one of the finest scenes in dramatic literature, she makes this heart-rending decision, and is fierce in the defense of Astyanax, only to have her hopes dashed by the cunning of Ulysses.

Andromacha retains enough spirit, nonetheless, to lash out sarcastically at Helen in the next act, and she maintains her regal and signified stature until hearing the crushing news that she had been awarded to Pyrrhus and that Astyanax is dead.

Of these two characters Andromacha is the more faceted and nuanced, but Hecuba is the more Senecan. The old queen undergoes that inner pain born of a consciousness of one's evil-producing condition, a consciousness that distinguishes a focal Senecan character. Andromacha, marvelous creation though she may be (and one whose character will furnish several traits to Racine), is not imbued with this type of awareness, principally because there can be only one "responsible" person in a tragedy by Seneca.

Medea

Medea is the most extraordinary of all the Senecan characters. As has been pointed out in Chapter I, Medea attracts all the attention, and thus is structurally closer to Hercules than to Andromacha or Hecuba.

Another similarity to Hercules lies specifically in her superhuman nature. However, she gives evidence of profound and varied emotion and never presents the almost wooden image that Hercules often does. Moreover, Medea's self-confidence and stature grow geometrically as the action proceeds, so that her vengeance cannot possibly be halted or deterred.

At first she seeks revenge, and goads herself to its accomplishment through jealousy. But the unfortunate queen is still so enamoured of Jason that she is willing to pardon him just as, for the same reason, Roxane will give Bajazet several opportunities to clear himself of suspicion. But when she determines to act, no form of argument can dissuade her. She will act, even alone, for she knows her own tremendous power, ready to be unleashed. And so she pronounces the famous lines (166-167), to be imitated with great effect in Corneille's *Médée*,[2] "Medea superest, hic mare et terras vides / ferrumque et ignes et deos et fulmina," ["Medea is left — in her thou beholdest sea and land, and sword and fire and gods and thunderbolts."]

Once her decision has been made, Medea is generally unshakable in her resolution for wide-sweeping revenge, and when Jason's weak point is discovered, she strikes home. She obviously enjoys evil and constantly seeks the supreme crime, but she does hesitate before the deed, as do many of Seneca's figures. Indeed, the momentary hesitation, the wavering, the character's struggle with himself recurs in Seneca's repertory, and this indecision underlines dramatically the note of personal responsibility for evil. In Christian terms, it is the notion of sufficient reflection and full consent of the will as prerequisites to assumption of complete responsibility. For, once the indecision has been overcome, the Senecan character always vows to fulfill his vicious intent, and then proceeds.[3]

In her passion, Medea has a vision of the Furies and her brother, demanding revenge. The device of the vision, dream, or hallucination reappears not infrequently in Seneca as an externalization of the disorder of the character's mind. At this point

---

[2] *Médée*, Act I, scene 5:
    Nérine: Dans un si grand revers que vous reste-t-il?
    Médée: Moi:
        Moi, dis-je, et c'est assez...
        Oui, tu vois en moi seule et le feu et la flamme,
        Et la terre et la mer, et l'enfer et les cieux,
        Et le sceptre des rois et la foudre des dieux.

[3] Concerning freedom and responsibility in *Phaedra*, J.-M. Croisille has perceptively noted ("Lieux Communs...," *Revue des Etudes Latines*, LXII [1964], 290): "... dans une perspective Stoïcienne, l'homme est loin d'être entièrement libre, [...] sa liberté est limitée par des données auxquelles il peut accorder ou refuser son assentiment, mais sur ce fond de fatalité se détache la responsabilité des personnages principaux: Phèdre, Hippolyte, Thésée. Il faut comprendre que le destin auquel pense Sénèque laisse à l'individu sa liberté de choix entre les possibles qu'il lui offre." This analysis applies to all of Senecan tragedy.

it is especially effective, since it demonstrates all the more clearly the deranged state of the enchantress.

After slaying one child to satisfy her brother, Medea proceeds to distinguish between a crime (accomplished) and vengeance (incomplete). She draws herself up to her fullest stature, achieves her revenge, and departs victorious, leaving humanity defeated. A recent writer has noted, to the point: "The pain and evil in much of the Greek tragedy is that of a broken order; Senecan tragic character, at its most vivid, is seen to grow and become more iron in a world of final disorder." [4]

Phaedra

Phaedra, after Medea, remains the most outstanding feminine figure in Senecan drama. Seneca makes us witness to her passion, its progress, its delirium, explosion, weakness, then eventually to its vengeance, remorse, and tragic end. It is in *Phaedra* that Seneca most vividly depicts the clash of passion and reason, with the former undermining and eventually overwhelming the latter. Thus the focus stays on the various stages of Phaedra's criminal love, to which is subordinated the fate of Hippolytus and the emotional difficulties of Theseus.

From the outset Phaedra freely admits that her greatest concern is an inner torment, an uncontrollable passion (cf. 101-103, 127-128). It is, in fact, this suppressed love which bursts forth in the Hippolytus — Phaedra confrontation, where the queen confesses all, ending her torrid declaration with the famous "miserere amantis." Here she is most satisfied and most humiliated, for her desire has found an outlet in expression, yet Hippolytus' reaction has reduced her to begging for pity. When Hippolytus draws his sword, Phaedra, from obviously masochistic motives, is thrilled at the thought of dying by his hand and she eagerly seeks annihilation. Hippolytus only adds to her frustration by denying her this and fleeing. The nurse then gathers up the sword dropped by the prince in his disgust. The stratagem of the sword proves to be one of the original devices that Seneca introduces into the Phaedra story.

---

[4] Charles Garton, "The Background to Character Portrayal in Seneca," *Classical Philology*. LIV, 1959, 5.

At Hippolytus' exit, Phaedra is left dazed, inanimate, crushed by shame and frustration. It is at Theseus' return that a change is discerned in Phaedra: her passion revealed, she has composed herself, become rather hard, in fact. Without a direct accusation, she coolly leads Theseus to conclude that his son is guilty. And so the victim of a harsh, inherited destiny that rendered its object sympathetic by the struggle she fought has now turned into a more rational, calculating type, seeking equally to protect and avenge herself.

The denouement finds a Phaedra both emotionally and psychologically destroyed by the death of Hippolytus and her own inability to quiet her love. She admits her guilt, and, with what must be Hippolytus' sword, commits suicide in a last passionate desire to rejoin the late prince. An interesting point is that Seneca avoids the use of the word "incest" throughout the entire tragedy, until, immediately before her death, Phaedra cries (1184-1185), "Morere, si casta es, viro; / si incesta, amori," ["Now die, if thou art pure, for thy husband's sake; if impure, for thy love."] Doubt still exists, therefore, as to whether Seneca considered Phaedra's desire as incestuous in itself, or rather adulterous and unchaste.

Phaedra is one of Seneca's finer portrayals, but he does not seem to have drawn greatly upon the Euripidean conception. Seneca has created her powerful, vigorous, passionate to the point of lacking the dignity and the femininity of the Greek counterpart.

Moreover, except in the scene where she calumniates Hippolytus, Phaedra is as sympathetic a character as may be found in Seneca, because of her suffering, caused by Hippolytus, prolonged by the nurse, and increased by the return of Theseus and subsequent events. She may yield to her passion, take pleasure in it, lie and slander, but she also struggles vainly against her instincts in the awful knowledge of the moral abyss into which she has plunged. She thus furnished the model for Racine's Phèdre, and perhaps even before Phèdre, for Roxane.

Atreus

The character Atreus and the Thyestean banquet have always represented revenge tragedy at the most horrible, and, in view of

Seneca's penchant for evoking horror, it is not surprising that the Roman dramatist composed what has come to be the only extant antique drama on that subject. When Atreus is first seen, he is already a vile person, and his criminal character seems so innate that it remains difficult to believe that he has recently evolved to this condition through a desire for revenge. Even in listing the crimes of Thyestes, Atreus gains no sympathy, because of his completely ruthless attitude. His thirst for vengeance knows no bounds, and he seeks to perform a crime to surpass all others.

Atreus proves bent enough on vengeance to be able to calm himself the better to calculate the suitable means. But, in the contemplation of various punishments, his sadism is excited; he goes mad and catches a glimpse of the Furies. He decides to deceive Thyestes, and to lure him into a trap.

The next time Atreus appears, he is expressing a kind of fiendish joy because Thyestes has taken the bait. [5] Atreus seeks revenge as profoundly as Medea, but his wrath does not have the world-shaking scope of hers. In perfect hypocrisy, finally, he pleads with his brother to share his title and goods. For Atreus revenge constitutes a science, a vile game, and he is extremely conscious of his role, which he throughly enjoys, even lengthening it by playing with Thyestes before he strikes home.

The audience learns the inevitable conclusion of Atreus' evolution through the recital of the murders. Seneca depicts him as a savage beast in human form, ripping and slashing at its victims. However, the following scenes, where he laughs at the ominous portents, grimly jokes with his brother, and still feels unsatisfied in his vengeance, prove even more revolting, for they are the epitome of the worst in human nature. The animal, irrational deed is less frightening than the calculated, more subtle human act.

Needless to add, his distasteful humor, his revelation of the disgusting truth, and his ultimate crushing of Thyestes into a state of despair do not elevate Atreus in our estimation: he is Seneca's incarnation of hatred.

---

[5] Seneca's Atreus, like Néron in Racine, takes pleasure in cruelty. The Racinian conception is modern, however, in the way physical desire and cruelty are linked in a kind of sadism.

Oedipus

The title-character of *Oedipus* is also the play's uncontested main figure. From the first lines Oedipus reveals himself as troubled by things unknown, suspicious, indeed certain that he is somehow responsible for the plague. The real nature of his acts is uncovered only gradually throughout, with sufficient events of double meaning to afford spells of hope and momentary relief.

The scene wherein Creon explains Laius' pronouncements to Oedipus contributes significantly to Seneca's characterization of the king, especially in these verses (668-670):

> iam iam tenemus callidi socios doli:
> mentitur ista praeferens fraudi deos
> vates, tibique sceptra despondet mea.
>
> ["No! now we see these two confederates
> Deep in a crafty plot: that priest of thine
> With lying tongue pretends the will of heaven,
> And promises my sovereignty to thee."]

Oedipus does not wish to believe Creon, because he cannot accept what he has feared most throughout — namely, his own responsibility for evil.

At about verse 764 ("Curas revolvit animus et repetit metus" ["My soul is filled with dark, foreboding fear; ..."]), Oedipus' suspicions begin to assume an air of credibility, and Jocasta unwittingly verifies them, only to have the inevitable postponed by the announcement of the death of Oedipus' "father" in Corinth. The hero still fears the second part of the oracle (incest), and it is in persistently seeking the answer to this problem that he runs headlong into the truth of his terrible fate (875-878):

> saeculi crimen vagor,
> odium deorum, iuris exitium sacri,
> qua luce primum spiritus hausi rudes
> iam morte dignus.
>
> ["The plague spot of the age, I wander here,
> Heaven-cursed pollutor of all sacred ties;
> Who, in the day when first I breathed the air,
> Was doomed to death."]

CHARACTERS   39

Since the oracle of Apollo has been fulfilled, Oedipus bitterly exclaims that now, at least, he can do no more harm. Yet he ultimately surpasses his impious destiny by being the cause, in a way, of Jocasta's suicide. So strong is his sense of personal guilt that he will depart from Thebes, taking upon himself the responsibility for all the evil.

Clytemnestra

Clytemnestra demonstrates once again that Seneca's most sensitive creations are his women. Though not approaching Medea's magnitude, Clytemnestra is similar in that she grows throughout the drama, becoming increasingly hard, resolute, ruthless.

Clytemnestra's shame, fear, and consequent indecision fill the play's first episode. She strives to persuade herself to act, to plunge deeper into evil, adulteress that she is, to be bold like Medea, more criminal than Helen (108-109, 114-115):

> Quid, segnis anime, tuta consilia expetis?
> quid fluctuaris? clausa iam melior est: ...
> da frena et omnem prona nequitiam incita:
> per scelera semper sceleribus tutum est iter.
>
> ["Why, sluggish soul, dost thou safe counsel seek?
> Why hesitate? Closed is the better way ....
> Loose be thy reins, swift speed thy wanton course;
> The safest way through crime is by the path
> Of greater crime."]

Yet a wounded modesty and a sense of guilt prevent her.

She continues in this very genuine state of hesitation, afraid for herself, enraged at Agamemnon's treatment of Iphigenia, jealous of her husband's new conquests, until her nurse finds the means to be encouraging. When Aegisthus makes his appearance, Clytemnestra is on the verge of submission and confession to the imminently expected Agamemnon. Aegisthus attempts to incite her to anger, but she directs it at him. Finally, however, the queen chooses adultery and murder rather than repentance.

From this point forward, the development of Clytemnestra's self-confidence and resolution becomes increasingly evident. Indeed, it is Clytemnestra (Cassandra tells us), who performs the axe-slaying of Agamemnon. And so this Lady Macbeth in reverse, at first weak, now brutally rock-solid, has evolved to the point of being more vicious and virile than Aegisthus.

Blood-stained and wild-eyed, she returns on stage to pronounce a harsh condemnation of Cassandra, and to have her own daughter imprisoned for life. The knowledge that Orestes has escaped does not dispel the notion that Clytemnestra has won the day, and with it at least temporary impunity.

Now that the major characters have been examined, we may profitably proceed to an analysis of what is tragic about a Senecan figure, and the best means to this end will consist in an investigation of the catastrophe of each play.[6] For, in determining where the catastrophe lies, one discovers that which was of greatest value to the protagonist and which, in order to cause the tragic pain, was placed in the most imminent peril.

In the *Hercules Furens* the tragedy lies, as I have suggested, not in the death of the family (which is catastrophic), but in Hercules' recognition of his own guilt and defeat, in a sense, by Juno. The same is true for *Hercules Oetaeus*, in which the hero suffers a tremendous blow to his pride in his own invincibility — suffers superhumanly until informed that fate, and not simply a more powerful creature, caused his downfall.

As in the two former plays, the tragic of the *Troades* has something to do with a knowledge of personal responsibility for evil. The catastrophe of the twin deaths of Astyanax and Polyxena functions as a final emotional fracturing of Hecuba, who considers herself the human cause. What was of greatest value to her (her personal dignity and the safety of her relatives) has been destroyed.

In *Medea*, the tragedy consists in the woman Medea's becoming, by her awful deeds, the legendary Medea: a deranged murderess. The slaughter of the children is indeed catastrophic, but not for Medea. Yet the revenge motive was introduced because the enchantress wanted to repay a flouting, an humiliation, an

---

[6] The *Phoenissae* exempts itself from this investigation by its abbreviated condition.

attack against her pride and conception of self.[7] In protecting her self-integrity, Medea fulfills the idea she has of her own stature. Therefore, self-fulfillment lies at the basis of Medea's plottings, much in the same way as in Racine's Néron.

An analogous instance may be found in *Agamemnon,* in which the title character's death functions as the catastrophe. But the principal figure, Clytemnestra, is motivated by a fear of being replaced by Cassandra, and also of being punished by Agamemnon. She plainly seeks to avoid humiliation or death, and commits her crime with impunity, growing increasingly vicious throughout in an attempt to assure self-preservation.

Preservation of self is also involved in *Oedipus.* The title figure is vitally concerned with saving himself from the evil destiny predicted for him,[8] and he is truly tragic when realizing his part in both the public and family disorders. Though he experiences all the despair of his guilt, Oedipus, like Hercules,

---

[7] Some critics have viewed *Medea* as a study in anger *(ira)* and its outward manifestations. (See Berthe Marti, "Seneca's Tragedies. A New Interpretation," *TAPA* LXXVI [1945], 216-245.) I rather think that the outbursts of wrath are means to the end of exposing Medea's fundamental desire for self-integrity, a desire which, in my analysis, is felt by the other major figures of Senecan tragedy. J.-M. Croisille ("Lieux communs," 300-301) seems to share my point of view, with particular reference to *Phaedra:* "Quant à l'intention profonde de Sénèque, dans la pièce, elle est de montrer justement, par l'exemple, comment la passion, dont l'individu est responsable, parvenant à son paroxysme, *tend à détruire cet individu* [italics mine] et à provoquer la ruine de son entourage. Si par surcroît, cet entourage répond à la passion par des réactions elles-mêmes passionées, la catastrophe devient inéluctable, et tout finit dans l'horreur."

[8] Concerning the struggle against destiny, Kastner and Charlton have observed *(Poetical Works,* p. xxxvi): "... it is a measure of Seneca's inferiority that his characters, unlike their Greek prototypes, are not fashioned as the typical human elements of a comprehensive universal scheme. Yet precisely this separation gives them a greater show of individuality. In their habitual role of strivers against Fate, they exhibit a mighty demoniacal power which gives apparent substance to this show; and in the hands of a rhetorician practising a form which offers little scope for action they inevitably reveal themselves through an analytic introspective utterance which completes the impression of a formal psychological portrait." Generally speaking, Kastner and Charlton are right. There is in Senecan theater, however, more action than has been credited to it. It need not be considered closet drama.

cannot be objectively regarded as totally responsible. Yet his integrity has been undermined, and he falls.

Phaedra is a guilty, responsible, tragic person. The fullness of the tragedy strikes her when Hippolytus' death (the catastrophe) is made known, for then she is supremely tormented by the death of the loved one, and by guilt for her fatal deception. The tragedy arises from Phaedra's very nature, for its basis lies in her criminal (and frustrated) passion for her stepson, coupled with an element of self-pride, a natural desire not to degrade her reputation by permitting the truth to be exposed.

Finally, it is evident that the grisly events in *Thyestes* do constitute the catastrophe, but not the tragedy of the play. For the tragic aspect one must look to that point where Atreus rejoices in the full completion of his revenge (verses 1096-1098), for it is here that Atreus, to repay a personal affront and satisfy his insane craving, renders Thyestes tragic by disturbing his very foundations, shaking his personal morality and self-order by making him party to the most heinous of deeds (1096-1098):

> Atreus: Nunc meas laudo manus,
>   nunc parta vera est palma. perdideram scelus,
> *nisi sic dolores.* (my italics)
>
> ["Now do I praise my handiwork indeed;
> Now I have gained the palm of victory.
> My deed had failed entirely of its aim
> Didst thou not suffer thus."]

In general, then, man, according to Seneca, can be responsible for his evil acts, and indeed this responsibility furnishes the major part of the tragic torment. He can also be tortured unjustly by learning of an ill unwittingly committed. Moreover, as with the characters of French classical theater and Racinian tragedy in particular, Seneca's figures undergo no change or striking development. Pierre Grimal has observed, "... leur être étant donné, il ne peut évoluer, il est determiné une fois pour toutes et la seule conclusion est la mort." [9] Therefore Seneca, like Racine, is an

---

[9] Grimal, "Les Tragédies de Sénèque," p. 9.

"essentialist" dramatist, trapping his creations in a *huis clos* where efficacious, liberating action becomes impossible.

However, the vitally important note sounded in each one of the tragedies remains that of one's integrity as a motive for action, and the destruction of this as a tragic event. The attack on the most personal and cherished part of the individual's composition causes, in Seneca, that psychological pain which makes for a Senecan tragedy.

What, in conclusion, will be said of Seneca's dramatic rendering of character? What can be the basic principle of these colorless characters whose uniformity of language is extended so far as to eradicate social differences, but who nevertheless do furnish traits for Racine to emulate? Much of Seneca's characterization has aptly been described as deriving from "these practices of inference, extension, exaggeration. The strength of the method lies in giving body and circumstances to an *ethos,* and psychological depth." [10] Therein is revealed the essence of Seneca's conception of character. His main figures give the impression of "psychological depth" due to an acute awareness and appreciation of self, an element not particularly native to Greek tragedy, but indispensible to Stoic literature.

But this principle is not without its flaws, dramatically speaking. Because of the pyramidal structure, whereby the one or two figures at the top gain prominence (and no others), one often finds great exaggeration due to a preference for placing the exclusive focus on the principals; the vast majority of those roles below "major" status are unindividualized, purely functional, sticklike creations. Moreover, on account of the consistently elevated, grandiose tone of the language, these characters may appear to be less lifelike than they otherwise would. As indicated in the next chapter, a certain monotony of tone, and an unfortunately narrow interpretation of Senecan characterization were the most immediate and striking legacies of the Roman author to his emulators in sixteenth-century France.

---

[10] Garton, p. 7.

PART TWO

THE SENECAN TRADITION IN FRENCH
SIXTEENTH- AND SEVENTEENTH-CENTURY
TRAGEDY

THE SENECAN TRADITION IN FRENCH SIXTEENTH- AND SEVENTEENTH-CENTURY TRAGEDY

The sixteenth-century French dramatist seeking to give new life to the tragic drama had several sources from which to draw. There was, of course, Aristotle (an edition of whose *Poetics* was published in Paris in 1541) and there was also the Latin drama, as represented by Seneca. But within the two general domains of Greek and Latin dramaturgy, there existed many and varied treatises and tragedies which the Renaissance playwright might well have known. Warner Patterson, following Lanson, lists these "extra-Aristotelian" sources of early Renaissance dramatic doctrine: (1) Donatus, *De tragoedia et comoedia;* (2) Horace, *Ars Poetica;* (3) the comedies of Plautus and Terence (for formal details): (4) the tragedies of Seneca and their Neo-Latin and Italian imitations; (5) technical works, such as the Roman M. Vitruvius Pollio's *De architectura libri decem,* and the Italian Leone Battista Alberti's *De re aedificatoria* (1485).[1] However, the one source that definitely did shape the future of French Renaissance drama, as practiced in its flowering by Jodelle, Garnier, and Montchrestien, was Senecan tragedy.[2]

---

[1] *Three Centuries of French Poetic Theory,* I (Ann Arbor, 1935), 275-276.

[2] Printed editions of Seneca's tragedies appeared early in France, and especially Italy — first at Ferrara in 1484, to be followed, a year later, by a Parisian edition. Editions were published in Lyon in 1491, and again in Paris in 1498. About ten editions of the complete tragedies came out during the sixteenth century, as well as individual plays. Thus the oft-noted Senecan "availability" to Renaissance man is based as much on the easy procurement of his works as on his linguistic accessibility (in contrast to Greek dramatists).

The vogue of Seneca as the principal model for tragedians begins with the dramatists of the 1550's and continues throughout the century.[3] In this chapter I have accordingly set up two basic goals: to give a precise idea of Seneca's fate in French tragedy between 1550 and 1660, and to insist upon his lasting contributions to the genre, contributions that explain a great deal of what is to be found in Racinian drama.

The sixteenth-century dramatists wrote plays in the Senecan mold in view of public presentation.[4] Lanson's research has shown that, in addition to performances at court, there were many representations in schools, a few presentations in provincial chateaux, and a few either by bourgeois amateurs or touring professionals in the provinces.

The first adaptation of a Senecan drama was *Médée* by La Péruse (*c.* 1553). But evident Senecan characteristics can be traced in an even earlier tragedy: Jodelle's *Cléopâtre Captive* (1552?), generally acknowledged as the earliest example of an original French Renaissance tragedy.[5]

The first observation that one must make about Seneca-inspired Renaissance tragedy is that the French Senecans are even more fascinated with the word and less with the deed than their

---

However, even to suggest that the Greek playwrights and their interpreter, Aristotle, were ignored would surely be folly. As early as 1537 there was a French translation of Sophocles' *Electra* by Lazare de Baïf, who also translated Euripides' *Hecuba* seven years later. Thomas Sebillet, whose *Art poétique françois* (1548) is the first French treatise to call itself an "Ars Poetica," composed a translation of the *Iphigenia* of Euripides in 1549.

[3] The interest in Seneca was undoubtedly spurred on by — and, in turn, helped to create a desire for — French translations of Seneca's plays: translations were published during the second half of the century by Premierfaict, Toutain, Le Digne, Le Duchat, Le Poitevin Herbodeau, and Le Montois J. Yeuwain. Furthermore, several of the so-called "original" French tragedies of the Renaissance are little more than translations of Seneca.

[4] Therefore the French did not think that Seneca was strictly to be declaimed, or read. For a brief summary of Lanson's findings in this area, see *Esquisse d'une Histoire de la Tragédie Française* (Paris, 1954), pp. 27-35.

[5] Raymond Lebègue (*La Tragédie Française de la Renaissance* [Bruxelles, 1954], p. 27) notes that the composition of *Abraham Sacrifiant* of Théodore de Bèze antedates that of *Cléopâtre*. Bèze's play, however, was to be of little significance for the development of French regular tragedy.

model. *Cléopâtre Captive* is a prime example: nothing happens; everything is described.

In form the play is classical, having a prologue, consisting of an *argumentum* (which precedes all of Seneca's dramas) and a dedication; choral odes at the end of the first four episodes; and, of course, five acts. The first scene of the first act, moreover, contains the description of his own downfall by "l'Ombre d'Antoine" who has just ascended from hell. His prediction of Cléopâtre's death before the day's end follows the typically Senecan device for creating suspense.

In Act I, scene 2, Cléopâtre expresses her longing for death. She participates in stichomythia, complains, laments, and relates the horrible sight of the bloodied Antoine that she had in a "songe." The act ends with the chorus generalizing on the brevity of happiness.

Act II introduces new characters who discuss Cléopâtre's fate, while often looking back to what has already happened. Act III gives the queen more opportunity for self-pity, and is followed in the fourth episode by her suicide, her solution to the dilemma of enslavement at Rome or fidelity in death to Antoine. However, the deed takes place offstage, being recounted by the chorus. The following act is entirely superfluous as far as the plot is concerned. It consists of lamentations, [6] a few invocations, and several additional details, which, though of no importance to the action,

---

[6] The lament-filled episodes of Seneca-inspired Renaissance tragedy are quite revealing, for they show that the sixteenth-century authors really understood the Stoic point of view which dictates that non-Stoic elements (such as violence, disorder and loud complaint) must dominate if the dramatist is to portray what happens when passion overwhelms reason. Julien-Eymard d'Angers has pointed out, in "Le Renouveau du Stoicisme au XVIe et au XVIIe siècle" (*Actes du VIIe Congrès de l'Association Guillaume Budé, 1963*, [Paris, 1964], 122-153), the high favor and extensive reading which Seneca's philosophical works enjoyed in the sixteenth and early seventeenth centuries. Later in the seventeenth century, Chapelain will see a contrast in the conduct and theories of Seneca himself: "Cependant je ne suis pas marry de voir que vous tombez d'accord que Sénèque avoit plus de théorie que de pratique en matière de philosophie stoïque et je ne desespère pas que vous n'en veniez un jour à l'opinion que j'ay commune avec quelques anciens et modernes, que la sagesse estoit toute sur sa langue et que son cœur estoit un cœur de commun." (*Lettre à M. de Balzac*, 24 décembre, 1639.)

do furnish Jodelle with the opportunity to display more of his stylistic wares.

The total effect of this play is that of eviscerated Seneca. Jodelle has deprived his drama of the tension, the action, most of the basic suspense, and all of the violence which characterize the Senecan play. Surely Senecan elements abound: an intense concentration on one character (who finds herself in somewhat of an "Andromacha" situation); a great deal of introspection and self-pity; long speeches in rhetorical, high-sounding language (Seleuque describes, almost preciously, Cléopâtre's slap, "Et de son poing mon visage empiré"). The use of anaphora even exceeds Seneca's in its abundance, and *sententiae* are found in considerable number. The "dream" device and the use of a chorus and a ghost also recall Seneca.

Thematically, too, *Cléopâtre Captive* follows a Senecan pattern. Revenge, death and suicide, captivity, passion, politics, and tragic destiny, however, play roles subsidiary to those of self-knowledge and suffering. This is logical, since these last two furnish the opportunity for the lengthy declamation that is the core of the play.

The major defect of this type of tragedy lies in the attempt, by Jodelle and his successors, to outdo Seneca at one aspect of his own game: in concentrating on rigid form and the dignified expression of tragic sentiment, the Renaissance dramatists of France chose to imitate the most obvious and least dramatic aspects of Seneca. And so, what is lacking in *Cléopâtre Captive* is simply life. Jodelle's imitation of Seneca has produced not an energetic reshaping of the action but a poor counterfeit. The only way events are presented is through a recitation of them, and if the characters do speak a great deal, they do not avail themselves of this opportunity to individualize themselves. Character analysis is negligible. *Cléopâtre Captive* fails badly as a dramatic conception because there is no drama: everyone, starting with the queen herself, remains passive and static.

Finally, Jodelle's play typifies French Renaissance tragedy in its late starting point. Seneca begins his dramas very close to the climactic moment so that emotions are extreme at the outset of the play. Jodelle's tragedy really begins *after* the principal event and looks back to it throughout. Thus, even the death of Cléopâtre has the negative value of a "fading away" rather than a positive and meaningful act. Remarkably, many of the crude Senecan devices found in *Cléopâtre Captive* reappear in Racine's theater (e.g., the dream, stichomythia, rhetorical expression). However, the refinement and revitalization effected by Racine and his predecessors succeed in changing the entire effect, and also in disguising the true (Senecan) source of some Racinian techniques.

The 1559-1563 period furnishes no less than six authors whose works betray the varied forms that Senecan inspiration was capable of taking: biblical [7] (*Aman*, 1559-60, by André de Rivaudeau, and *Saül le furieux*, 1562, by Jean de La Taille), historical-exotic (*César*, 1560, of Jacques Grévin, and *La Soltane*, 1561, by Gabriel Bounin), mythological (*Achille*, 1563, by Nicolas Filleul), plus a direct translation of Seneca's *Agamemnon* in 1561 by Le Duchat.[8] The theme of vengeance, divine and otherwise, links the original creations, and the Senecan treatment of this subject (as seen usually in *Medea* and *Thyestes*) evidently influenced the dramatists in question, even in the rather irregular offering by Bounin, which is, nonetheless, a version of the Medea legend.

By far the outstanding play of this cluster, for my purposes as well as for Renaissance dramatic theory, is *Saül le furieux*. In his preface, "De l'Art de la Tragédie," Jean de La Taille defines the genre in this fashion: "Son vray subject ne traicte que de piteuses ruines des grands Seigneurs, que des inconstances de Fortune, que bannissements, guerres, pestes, famines, captivitez, execrables cruautez des Tyrans: et bref, que larmes et miseres extremes... car il faut que le subiect en soit si pitoyable et poignant de soy, qu'estant mesmes en bref et nument dit, engendre en nous quelque passion: comme qui vous conteroit d'un à qui lon fit malheureusement manger ses propres fils, de sorte que le

---

[7] Renaissance tragedy uses historical, mythical, and biblical backgrounds, the last being an evident reflection of the taste for and turbulence in things religious during the sixteenth century. In the ensuing century plays with biblical themes will constitute a very small minority indeed.

[8] Undoubtedly a sizable impetus was given to the already considerable preference for Seneca by the publication of Scaliger's *Poetics* in 1561. Scaliger draws upon several sources, but his practical model for tragedy, and for its sententious, declamatory style, is Senecan drama.

Pere (sans le sçavoir) seruit de sepulchre à ses enfans...." [9] The definition could fit none other but a Senecan conception of tragedy, and the concrete example makes it conclusive, for *Thyestes* is a properly Senecan play having no dramatic equivalent in extant classical literature. Furthermore, La Taille proceeds to name the tragedies of Seneca as models worthy of imitation. [10]

Although the period 1570-1585 saw the publications of the works of Robert Garnier, the appearance of other plays shaped in the Senecan mold must not be overlooked. Jean de La Taille continued his imitation of Seneca in *La Famine* of 1573; Chantelouve composed *La Tragédie de feu Gaspard de Coligny* about 1575; Robelin offered his rendition of the Theban story, *La Thébaïde*, in 1584; and in 1585 Jean-Edouard Du Monin wrote a French adaptation of the *Orbecche* of Cinthio, entitled *Orbecc-Oronte*, about which Elliot Forsyth has succintly commented, "Sujet, forme, psychologie, pensée, tout, en effet, rappelle ici les tragédies de vengeance du dramaturge latin." [11]

The same may be said, to a great extent, about Garnier's tragedies. His imitation of Seneca is quite close at times, but less apparent at others. In Garnier's generation, the ghost, heretofore considered a good theatrical device, is felt to be generally incompatible with tragic dignity, as is the presentation of death or violence on stage: Seneca-inspired tragedy has undergone a kind of modernization, a step in the direction of Racinian drama.

However, the lofty style of Seneca makes itself felt even more in Garnier. Garnier's contribution to the evolution of the tragic genre consists in his successful incorporation of beautiful verse within the usual Senecan framework. Heretofore, the language of tragedy in France was constructed largely to produce power and emotional impact, with little regard for the poetic quality of the verse. Garnier brought a supple, exquisite poetry to French tragedy while still maintaining the elevated tone. Like Jodelle, however, he worked on the stylistic aspect to the detriment of the action.

---

[9] *Jean de La Taille und sein Saül le Furieux*, ed. Dr. A. Werner (Leipzig, 1908), p. 10.
[10] *Ibid.*, p. 12.
[11] *La Tragédie Française de Jodelle à Corneille* (Paris, 1962), p. 258.

For example, the *Argument* preceding *Cornélie* (printed in 1573) contains both long and full description of action that has already occurred.[12] And so the play itself is a *reflection* on the past. Indeed, Cicéron opens the first act in a monologue, in a lament for the dead, which is simply too long. This sort of lamentation runs throughout the entire play, whose focus, however, remains almost exclusively on Cornélie. Her feeling of guilt for the death of Pompée and her self-pity fill much of the first two acts, which close, as usual, with a choral pronouncement.

In Act III, Cornélie relates the awful dream she had the night before, then engages in the first bit of impassioned dialogue encountered in the play. Act IV represents a change of interest, for the conspirators against the emperor, as well as César and Antoine, are seen and heard. As the episode ends, a "chœur de Césariens" expresses hope for César's safety. The use of a chorus whose title betrays its sympathies is rare at this point in French tragedy, and probably represents Garnier's attempt at tightening tragedy by bringing the chorus into something of an effective relationship with the principals.

In as Senecan a scene as can be conceived, a messenger opens Act V by relating the valiant death of Scipion, father of Cornélie. Cornélie's reaction, an excellent example of Senecan invocation, is:

> O dieux cruels! ô ciel! ô frères destinées!
> O soleil lumineux qui dores nos journées!
> O flambeaux de la nuit pleins d'infélicitez![13]

She states that she will live just long enough to lament properly her husband and father and that then she will join them.

---

[12] Just as the relative abundance of biblical subjects betrayed the preoccupations of an earlier generation, the plays of Garnier which treat civil upheaval, such as *Cornélie* and *Marc Antoine,* reflect the dominant concern of the 1570's.

[13] Passages such as this immediately recall Boileau's deriding remarks in the *Art Poétique* (III, v. 135-140):

> Que devant Troie en flamme Hécube désolée
> Ne vienne pas pousser une plainte ampoulée,
> Ni sans raison décrire en quels affreux pays
> Par sept bouches l'Euxin reçoit le Tanaïs.
> Tous ces pompeux amas d'expressions frivoles
> Sont d'un déclamateur amoureux des paroles.

Cornélie's plight resembles Hecuba's in that both are in unfortunate positions at the start of the play and their fortunes grow worse. The best they can do is to complain of their harsh fate. Gustave Lanson's definition of Renaissance tragedy fits *Cornélie* perfectly, "un drame pathétique qui tire l'émotion non de la vue directe du fait tragique, mais de la plainte des victimes." [14]

Hippolyte represents Garnier as a playwright more favorably, for this tragedy does indeed possess a dramatic interest. The inner tension which holds *Cornélie* together is caused by the event which has occurred before the start of the drama itself. In *Hippolyte* the tension proceeds from the dramatic nature of the situation, and we should credit Garnier with retaining the essential features of the Senecan *Phaedra* as the core of his own play. It is, in fact, in the strictly original segments of *Hippolyte* that the drama loses its edge.

As was the case with *Cornélie*, *Hippolyte* displays a considerable quantity of Senecan techniques. [15] The very first scene of the play, in which the "Ombre d'Egée" comes up from hell to predict the deaths of the three principal figures, was most likely conceived with *Agamemnon* in mind. There are two choruses, a good deal of dramatic irony, a nurse who acts as *confidente* to Phèdre. Hippolyte, too, describes dreams he has had.

But the evident debt to Seneca is in entire scenes borrowed directly from the Latin dramatist. In fact, the whole of Act II is of Senecan conception, with many of Seneca's speeches translated and put to good use by Garnier. [16]

The conception of characters differs slightly from Seneca's. The French Hippolyte could not be expected to be as rough-hewn or

---

[14] *Esquisse*, p. 21.

[15] The influence of Euripides' *Hippolytus* is negligible in Garnier. As Raymond Lebègue says of Renaissance dramatists in general (*Tragédie Française de la Renaissance*, p. 18), "... nos dramaturges ne demandaient au théâtre grec qu'un appoint, un complément de ce que leur fournissait leur principal modèle: Sénèque."

[16] In *De Jodelle à Molière* (Paris, 1911), pp. 73-78, Rigal reviews the nature and extent of Garnier's debt to Seneca in *Hippolyte*. He does not point out the frequent appearance in *Hippolyte*, as elsewhere in Garnier, of animal imagery derived from Seneca. Racine, on the other hand, studiously avoids such figures.

antisocial as the Roman, but Phèdre bears a strong resemblance to her Latin counterpart. As in Seneca, though not in Euripides, the tragedy is centered on her. In fact, *Hippolyte* forms part of a chain of French classical tragedies which focus on the Phèdre theme from a basically Senecan point of view.[17] The play is not a complete success, for the length of Garnier's discourses necessarily slows the pace of the action. But he does express sentiment in a rich and elegant style reminiscent of Seneca. Indeed Garnier brought the first truly poetic talent to French Renaissance tragedy.

Apart from his own personal affinity for Seneca, Garnier remains invaluable to any discussion of the Senecan tradition because of his influence on dramatists of the ensuing fifty years. Through imitation of his works, Senecan techniques will reappear in tragedies of the first third of the seventeenth century.

Between 1585 and 1630 Seneca's dramatic fortunes in France took two distinct routes. First, he served as the continuing preferred model for classical form and moral theme. On the other hand, his violent side was appreciated, for the first time, and helped to create those plays of the period not in the classical mold, sometimes known as "baroque."[18]

A whole cluster of plays that recall Seneca were printed between 1589 and 1599, six of them in 1589 alone. Owing to the example of Garnier, several authors turned to Senecan subjects, with varying results. While it is basically the conception of the revenge theme which marks François Perrin's debt to Seneca in *Sichem ravisseur* (1589), the affiliation of Guillaume Regnault, Pierre Matthieu, and Roland Brisset has a broader basis. The very

---

[17] Winifred Newton, in *Le Thème de Phèdre et d'Hippolyte dans la Littérature Française*, discusses the plays built around the Phaedra story. See also Jean Pommier, *Aspects de Racine* (Paris, 1954), André Stegmann, "Les Métamorphoses de Phèdre," *Actes du Premier Congrès International Racinien* (Uzès, 1962) pp. 43-52, and my note "Un Précurseur méconnu de *Phèdre: Béral Victorieux de Borée,*" *RHL*, LXV, No. 1 (jan.-mars 1965), 103-107.

[18] I do not intend to furnish a list of all the plays with Senecan traces which belong to either category ("classical," "baroque") during the 1585-1630 period. For my purposes, it will suffice merely to show that the Senecan tradition remained alive in both domains. Moreover, Elliott Forsyth has already accomplished the useful task of categorizing most of the dramas of the span in question. (See *La Tragédie Française de Jodelle à Corneille*, pp. 251-325).

title of *La Tragédie d'Octavie femme de l'empereur Néron* (1589) by Regnault betrays its (pseudo-) Senecan subject matter. Brisset's debt is more profond, for his plays come very close to being servile translations of the Senecan counterparts: *Hercules Furieux, Thyeste, Agamemnon,* and *Octavie.* In addition, almost all the *pièces liminaires* to the 1589 text of Brisset's works refer (1) to France's political difficulties as the reason for the resurgence of the tragic spirit and (2) to Seneca's influence on Brisset. For example, in the "Sonet de Monsieur d'Amb. Sr. de Vezeui" one encounters this statement:

> L'Aygle épreuve au soleil les petits de son ayre:
> Sénèque est ton FEBUS, où tu vas animant
> De ton fecond esprit le prompt enfantement.

Brisset's versions are but pale imitations of the original, but they remain less insufferable than those of Matthieu *(La Guisade* and *Clytemnestre,* 1589), because Brisset succeeds in capturing some of Seneca's finer points (inevitably, since his plays are virtually mere translations), while Matthieu's freer interpretations miss the mark entirely. This is not to deny that Matthieu was aware of Senecan techniques; on the contrary, his works abound in long monologues, ghosts, *songes, sententiae,* political considerations, violence and death. However, the shallowness of his character study and, in *Clytemnestre,* the painful moralizing of the "nourrice" distinguish his conception from Seneca's.

Brisset and Regnault reveal the continuing tendency to copy very closely, while Matthieu belongs to the increasing number who prefer a looser imitation. In the latter group belong Simon Belyard *(Le Guysien,* 1592), Luc Percheron *(Pyrrhe,* 1592), and Le Sieur Du Souhait *(Radegonde duchesse de Bourgogne,* 1599). Seneca's image still imposes itself upon those who, at this time, are creating "baroque" drama, but his works are looked to for more general treatments and conceptions. [19] This liberalization is a step forward in the development of Seneca-inspired drama from

---

[19] As indication that Seneca's influence is not seriously in danger of disappearing at this point, one may recall that in his *Art Poétique* of 1597 Delaudun d'Aigaliers rates Seneca higher than the Greeks.

the close adaptations of the early Renaissance to the successful absorption of Seneca in Racinian tragedy.

In view of what is to come, it might be well to reiterate that, between 1550 and 1600, Seneca's influence was exerted above all on the formal aspects of French tragedy: his plays were imitated for their structure of a tragic situation, based on renowned myths and legends and employing characters of great magnitude. A secondary reason for the emulation of Seneca lies in the nature of his content: the question of the rights and duties of royalty, frequently debated in a sententious manner by two principals, and the question of responsibility, so central to every major figure in Seneca, were of special interest to the dramatist and public alike of France between 1560 and 1600.

Between 1600 and 1610 French dramatic writing evidences a few attempts at innovation while retaining many traditional Senecan techniques. Abbé Nicolas de Montreux (*Sophonisbe*, 1601) includes the scene-opening monologues, the Stoic choral themes, the considerable amount of *sententiae*, and the expression of self-lamentation that could as well be discovered in a play of 1580. But the subject (quite reminiscent of Jodelle's *Cléopâtre Captive*) does not really come from Seneca, nor do certain relatively new elements: the absence of a choral intervention at the end of an act (IV), and the establishment of the dilemma, so dear to French tragedy of the Cornelian era — in this instance, Massinisse's struggle between personal and public interest.

In the revenge tragedy *Rosemonde* (1603) by Nicolas Chrestien des Croix, the nature of the subject imposes upon the author several time-tested Senecan procedures for creating suspense and insisting upon the foulness of the deeds (e.g., the appearance of supernatural beings in the prologue, moral themes enunciated by the chorus, forebodings of evil). None the less, Chrestien des Croix does not limit himself to the Senecan outline for a revenge play, and thus *Rosemonde* does not convey the same impression as a Brisset work, for example.

However, another play of the period does: *Alboin* (1610) by Claude Billard. [20] Here are all the Senecan techniques, from the

---

[20] Billard's *Polyxène* (1607) constitutes another good example of Senecan tragedy at this time.

use of ghosts (l'ombre de Totyle), interminably long soliloquies, and a moralizing, poorly integrated chorus, which closes each act, to the revenge theme, complete with violence and horror, obviously based on the Medea story. In fact Rosemonde expresses herself like Medea (Act V):

> Non, je me vangeray: si l'amour ne peut pas
> Me vanger par ta main [Elméchide], guide de mes appas,
> J'iray par l'univers, aux lieux plus solitaires
> Invoquer les Demons, les ombres mortuaires,
> Les Monstres, les Tyrans, les enfans depites
> De la terre animée, & mille cruautés,
> Pour me vanger, chetive, & boire insatiable
> Du sang de ce tyran....

The only element which has a prominence not typical of Seneca is the love plot, whose presence in a French tragedy should not be a source of surprise.

In tone and vocabulary, Montchrestien's *La Reine d'Escosse* belongs to the tradition begun by Jodelle, though the fluidity of its verse looks forward. Academic interest in literary form and moral content, particularly the morality of politics, also ties Montchrestien to the Renaissance.[21] However, in his choice of a modern subject, his attempt at integrating the chorus into the action of the play, and in his rather sensitive portrayal of a woman character, Montchrestien surpasses his predecessors. Most French dramas of Senecan inspiration fail to portray the convincing women characters found in Seneca; Montchrestien's portrayal of Marie Stuart is exceptional.

One can easily trace the evolution of Renaissance tragedy from Jodelle through Montchrestien because of the basic structural components found in these creations: a certain unity of tone and

---

[21] In his article ("Les Sentences et le 'but moral' dans les Tragédies de Montchrestien," *RSH*, 105 [janvier-mars, 1962], 5-14), Richard Griffiths cautions that it is unwise to conclude that a Renaissance dramatist (Montchrestien is Griffiths' example) was concerned with things moral merely because his *sententiae* apparently reflect such a preoccupation. Griffiths notes that the use of *sententiae*, among other rhetorical devices, is a technique for ornamentation of a work and thus the content may have little to do with the author's personal convictions.

action,[22] one deed of importance that causes profound psychological suffering, the exposition of points of view on political and moral tenets. Yet, we should quickly note that this type of drama was not to continue flourishing long, for between 1600 and 1630 the work of Alexandre Hardy came to dominate the dramatic scene. However, the Senecan influence was chiefly felt, during the first two decades of the seventeenth century, not by Hardy, but by Jean Prevost and Pierre Mainfray, two humanists who, in their desire to re-establish classical tragedy after the excesses of many of the "baroque" and romanesque plays of the preceding age, looked to Seneca for their model.[23]

Prevost's *Edipe* (1614) constitutes an attempt at an adaptation of the Senecan original, while remaining extremely faithful to the Latin text. The facts of the plot, the choral themes, the characterization, indeed the very manner of expression of the characters recall Seneca at every turn. Prevost particularly appreciated the moments of greatest emotion, as found in Seneca, and he translated them, as in Act V:

Edipe: O Phebus! ô trepieds! ô vous devineresses!
O Delphiques lauriers! vos voix sont menteresses!
Vous m'aviez une fois parricide prédit:
Mais je suis plus meschant que vous m'aviez dict.[24]

The other offering of Prevost which is of interest is *Hercule* (1613). Although inferior to *Edipe* from a stylistic point of view, *Hercule* displays as great a debt to Seneca. Indeed, Jacques Morel has called it "une traduction libre."[25]

Yet, as Morel has also seen, Prevost does make an effort at rendering to Seneca some of the dramatic life he possesses in the

---

[22] An effort was usually made to adhere to the unities. In these plays temporal allusions are very rare and so the dramas are, as it were, abstracted from time and space. Their unity is the unity of a void.

[23] An anonymous tragedy of this period also seems to have been influenced by Seneca, in particular *Medea: Tragédie françoise d'un more cruel* (1614?).

[24] Cf. v. 1044-1053 of *Oedipus*.

[25] "*L'Hercule sur l'Oeta* de Sénèque et les Dramaturges Français de l'époque Louis XIII," *Les Tragédies de Sénèque et le Théâtre de la Renaissance* (Paris, 1964), 98.

original and which had been ignored in the Renaissance. To this end, Prevost incorporates the violence typical of Seneca and even tries to make Stoic morality conform to the standards of seventeenth-century France. In itself, the work of Jean Prevost has little value, but it discloses an early seventeenth-century author's desire to bring authentic Senecan qualities back to the theatrical scene after their gradual decrease in popularity at the end of the sixteenth century.

Pierre Mainfray's version of a Senecan play has no merit whatsoever apart from its obvious borrowings from Seneca. *Tragédie des forces incomparables et amours du grand Hercules* (1616) is an irregular drama in four acts which combines elements from both *Hercules Furens* and *Hercules Oetaeus*, and interposes a basic element of Mainfray's own invention: the love theme of "vainqueur vaincu" concerning Hercules and Iolle. By eliminating the usual chorus and reducing the number of acts, Mainfray had perhaps thought of revitalizing the story as Seneca had told it. But Mainfray's creation remains lifeless and abstract, and perhaps his play's only saving grace is that it may well have contributed an element or two to Rotrou's *Hercule Mourant*.

Any claim to a continuous line of influence which passed through the early seventeenth century would be incomplete and invalid if it did not include the dramas of Alexandre Hardy. At the beginning of his career, Hardy tends towards subjects taken from antiquity, uses five acts, shows rhetorical training, and in general employs many of the techniques of his immediate predecessors. In fact, twelve of his extant plays have choruses. Moreover, Hardy is not above prolonging a play by a final act filled with lamentation. But none of his works consists entirely of verbal complaint. In point of fact, it is Hardy who definitely shifts the trend to the side of the *active* hero whose basic emotions are in conflict with those of another. In so doing, Hardy prepares the way for classical tragedy.

Hardy's debt to Seneca is much more subtle and indirect than either Prevost's or Mainfray's. In his *Scédase*, the first scene opens with the usual introductory monologue, and the purpose of the scene, besides exposition, is to sow the beginnings of suspense and expectation. The foreboding of evil carries over into the second act where Scédase's daughters, Euxipe and Théane, are concerned about the evil atmosphere which hovers around them. Up to this point the imitation of the Senecan type of drama is apparent.

The catastrophe then takes place in Act III when Charilas and Euribiade rape and strangle the girls. After the discovery of the bodies by the overwhelmed father (Act IV), there follows the final episode wherein Scédase, frustrated and enraged that the king will do nothing to bring the murderers to justice, hurls imprecations at Sparta and commits suicide. Scédase's torment is based on his incapability to have justice accomplished and his daughters avenged. But, in contrast to Senecan characters, he does not share any real responsibility for the terrible events, and thus his feeling of frustration cannot attain the status of a true tragic emotion.

Formally, the play makes no attempt at observing the unities. Its main figure is a bourgeois, a fact which immediately sets *Scédase* apart from the line of French classical tragedy, and which contributes to the application of the term "tragédie irrégulière" to *Scédase*. Moreover, the foul events of Act III, apparently presented in full view of the audience, constitute one of the most extreme violations of *bienséances* imaginable. An even more basic difference from his predecessors is discovered in the very conception of what constitutes a drama. Garnier, for example, portrays the emotional result of an event. Hardy portrays the event and its emotional result. With Racine, tragedy will discover the entire psychology of the hero and its effects on external events.

It might seem possible to conclude that, despite an occasional Senecan touch, Hardy appears to have completely broken away from the Latin author's influence. And yet, how complete is this divorce? For although he is not, strictly speaking, a "Senecan" dramatist, Hardy does have a definite Senecan trait here and there in his repertory. The externals of several of his dramas, though Senecan in great part, no doubt were brought to Hardy by the tradition, thus indirectly. These would include the preference for "sujets antiques," the monologues, the chorus, the *sententiae*, the themes of revenge and suffering, a certain didactic element,[26] the play-closing suicide, and finally that rhetorical form of expression (but not the unity of tone) which is common to French Renaissance tragedy.

Directly, Hardy probably borrowed select bits of Seneca. Jules Beraneck in his *Sénèque et Hardy* (Leipzig, 1890), indicates several instances of this. For example, Seneca's verses 60-61 of *Agamemnon*, "numquam placidam sceptra quietem, certumve sui tenuere diem" ["Never have sceptres obtained calm peace or certain tenure"], are rendered in Hardy's *Arsacome* (855-856) as "Le sceptre à quiconque le porte / File des périls infinis...." Or, compare *Oedipus*, 324, "libata Bacchi dona permutat cruor" ["Bacchus' gift poured out changes to blood"] with *Didon*, 1306 ff., "Le prêtre par trois fois d'horreur se recula / Voyant le vin sacré (chose fâcheuse à croire) / De pur sang devenu, prendre une couleur noire." And so Hardy apparently knew something of the true Seneca. Whether this was in the original Latin or through an intermediary such as Garnier is not clear, but the latter possibility seems to be the stronger.

In his later career, Hardy reduced and then suppressed the chorus, turned to modern subjects, and in general tightened his tragedy for the sake of action and to cater to the public taste. And yet, in *Alcméon*, a play posterior to *Scédase*, one discovers a revenge tragedy conceived along strikingly Senecan lines, especially as seen in *Medea*. Rigal has concluded: "On y trouve une apparition d'ombre, un songe, des présages, un récit final; chaque personnage important est flanqué d'une 'nourrice' ou d'un vieux serviteur; les monologues sont longs et nombreux, tandis que le dialogue prend volontiers une allure symétrique et sentencieuse; enfin les souvenirs et les noms de la mythologie abondent. Tout cela est du Garnier."[27] It is also *du Sénèque*.

And so, Seneca reappears even in the works of Alexandre Hardy, though admittedly in a more indirect than direct fashion. Because of the popularity of the tragicomedy, the pastoral, and the "baroque" plays during the first thirty years of the seventeenth

---

[26] Scédase's frequent allusions to the moral corruption of his century give rise to speculation that Hardy may have permitted himself to do some preaching in this particular work.

[27] *Alexander Hardy et le Théâtre Français* (Paris, 1889), p. 395.

century, the classical side of the Senecan tradition does not possess the strength it had in the sixteenth century. But with the new generation of dramatists that came to the fore in the 1630's, Seneca again takes his place as a major, direct influence.

Before passing on to Rotrou, I must mention two plays of the late 1620's which deserve credit at least for retaining in the dramatic corpus the most fascinating of all subjects of French tragedy: the Phaedra legend. *L'Innocence Descouverte* (1628) by Jean D'Auvray adds little to the evolution of the legend rendered popular in France under the aegis of Seneca. In fact, D'Auvray's play is little more than a re-edition of his *Marsilie* of 1609.

In 1627 Vincent Borée published four tragedies, one of which, *Béral victorieux*, contains two distinct plots. The significance of this play lies in the fact that the basic plot possesses the elements of the Phaedra drama (as treated by Garnier), barely hidden under the superimposed story of the valor of Béral, ancestor of the Prince de Piémont to whom the play is dedicated. Even more remarkable than the mere presence of the celebrated theme is the consideration that *Béral* is the forerunner of those French tragedies which will incorporate the story into a historical background as well as those which will keep its mythological cadre. Finally, certain aspects of Borée's play (the non-incestuous nature of the love, the use of an intermediary, the remorse of the queen) announce another road which the theme will take, that of the "tragédie épurée." [28]

Béral victorieux therefore forms the necessary link in the chain between Garnier's version (*Hippolyte*, 1573) and La Pinelière's (*Hippolyte*, 1635), and thus kept alive the Senecan rendition of a theme of major significance in anticipation of the day when regular tragedy was again to flower.

Around 1630 Seneca evidently commanded sufficient respect to be a source for the imminent renaissance of tragedy. Perhaps the ideas of Scaliger as promulgated by Daniel Heinsius in *De tragoediae constitutione* (Leyden, 1611) were responsible for rejuvenating Seneca at this time and throughout a major part

---

[28] *Béral's* position in literary history is given much fuller treatment in my article mentioned in note 17.

of the century. Also, just before *Hercule Mourant*, Benoît Bauduyn had assisted in spreading a knowledge of Seneca by publishing, in 1629, the first complete verse translation of the tragedies in French. The very next year would see the publication of the excellent *Traduction du Traité des Bienfaits de Sénèque* by Malherbe. Thus, when Rotrou seeks a model for his first tragedy, he naturally turns to Seneca. With *Hercule Mourant* (and the *Sophonisbe* of Mairet), *tragédie* [29] as a genre comes into its own for the first time.

An examination of the *Hercule Mourant* reveals a free adaptation, but with moments of close imitation, even translation, of Seneca's *Hercules Oetaeus*. However, unlike most of his Seneca-inspired predecessors, Rotrou knew how to imitate. Sensing that concision would be the shibboleth of the revitalized genre, he omitted the chorus, [30] reduced the longer speeches, redistributed the parts so that monologues and examples of stichomythia, though present, are less prominent, and generally gave more balance to the work by breathing life into Déjanire and Iole, thus making the play less "monocentric."

The work is, nevertheless, recognizably of Senecan inspiration, from the opening monologue (which occurs rather frequently in the first forty years of the century), through the revenge and madness themes, to the device of the magic potion. Yet Rotrou accomplishes a striking transformation of the Senecan characters: Hercules is no longer the towering, powerful braggart of Seneca,

---

[29] I use the French word *tragédie* to distinguish between the new genre as written by Rotrou and Mairet (and which demanded the inclusion of certain specific factors: three unities, the division into [five] acts and scenes, noble characters, unity of tone, elevated language, a plot passion and politics, the use of *alexandrins*, and the convention of the *liaison des scènes*) and that genre, practiced between 1550 and 1640 which, by its literary models, merits the title of French *classical* tragedy. It is, therefore, to avoid the confusion that has beset critical terminology (for example, Rotrou has been called "classic," "pre-classic," and "baroque") that I differentiate between (French classical) tragedy, and the new form *tragédie*, born c. 1632-34. I am indebted to the late Professor E. B. O. Borgerhoff for this helpful distinction.

[30] In the seventeenth century, the chorus is felt to be incompatible with tragedy's compactness, and the last important (non-religious) play to use one is Mairet's *Silvanire* of 1631.

but (as in Mainfray's version) a love struck conqueror made captive by passion, who even goes to his knees before Iole. He is thus the Hercules of the romance rather than of the epic tradition.

By the beginning of Act II Déjanire looms as a more terrible figure than Hercule, and jealousy will obviously play a key role. Iole, the captive, finds herself caught between Hercule's passion and Déjanire's vengeance while trying to protect Arcas, her lover. The character Iole reveals Rotrou's dramatic sense. She is the most genuine figure in her predicament and expression of emotions, and she owes the prominence of her role solely to Rotrou, for he gives her major status in *Hercule Mourant* as compared to the minor one she occupied in *Hercules Oetaeus*. Unfortunately, when Iole leaves the play, so does Rotrou's originality.

Therefore, as early as the beginning of Act IV, the play has lost most of its movement and becomes a vehicle for Hercule's verbal search for the identity of his conqueror. But this is not the soul-shattering, humiliating puzzlement of *Hercules Oetaeus*. By making of Hercule a romantic *salon-habitué*, Rotrou deprives him of his stature and thus his fall is unfortunate but not of profound or tragic consequence.[31]

Finally, a messenger enters to relate Déjanire's suicide, stating, "Déjanire à nos yeux, malgré notre défense / D'un ruisseau de son sang a lavé son offense." Hercule then learns the truth and Act IV ends with Philoctète's promise to slay Arcas. This last detail is essential because, recognizing the poor dramatic quality of Seneca's fifth act of *Hercules Oetaeus*, Rotrou decides to add something so that the plot will not be resolved until the end of the play, a technique that will mark French classical tragedy in its flowering, and in particular the suspenseful tragedies of Racine.

After the expected description of Hercule's death which opens Act V, there ensues an argument, purely of Rotrou's invention,

---

[31] Morel believes that Rotrou deformed the Senecan conception of the hero and made Hercule conform to a newer standard ("Hercule sur l'Oeta et les Dramaturges Français," p. 110): —"*L'Hercule Mourant* confirme qu'aux yeux de Rotrou, comme à ceux des 'généreux' ses contemporains, la grandeur des passions est signe d'une autre grandeur, celle de l'héroisme ou celle de la sainteté."

between Alcmène and Philoctète as to whether Arcas should be slain. Then, lightning is heard, the heavens open, and "Hercule, descendant du ciel," resolves the difficulty by pardoning Arcas.

The spectator's preoccupation, in *Hercule Mourant*, is with a hero, a personality who acts and is responsible. Although Rotrou's universe is more mobile in its activity and in the possibility of the occurrence of any number of events, the focus remains, as in Seneca, on Hercules.

It was probably during 1634 that the *Hippolyte* of La Pinelière was written, an evident imitation of Seneca. Lancaster has observed that *Hippolyte*'s significance lies in its support of Rotrou's notion that Seneca-inspired tragedy was stageworthy. [32] Thus the success of *Hercule Mourant* probably promoted La Pinelière, and others after him, to return once again to seeking out Seneca in the original Latin. Seneca, as a direct influence, had not been felt to any appreciable degree since the Renaissance tragedies, but with Rotrou he returns in force. In fact Rotrou uses Senecan subject matter once more, although to a lesser extent, in *Antigone* of 1638. This is not at all unusual, for, though there were only twelve tragedies based on ancient sources between 1635 and 1651, Seneca was the most copied. [33]

Pierre Corneille's first contribution to the domain of tragic drama, *Médée*, also reflects a knowledge of and admiration for Senecan subject and technique. In his attempt at staging Seneca *francisé*, Corneille comes very close to the spirit of the original, with the expected exceptions of those elements germane only to French tragedy. Indeed, of all the writers of the genre, Corneille *sounds* the most like Seneca. The reasons may become apparent through an examination of *Médée*.

---

[32] See *A History of French Dramatic Lit.*, (Baltimore, 1929-1942), part 1, II, 692. I will return to La Pinelière presently.

[33] 1635: *Médée* (Corneille), *Hippolyte* (La Pinelière); 1638: *Le Thyeste* (Monléon), *Antigone* (Rotrou); 1639: *L'Innocent Malheureux* (Grenaille), *Hercule Furieux* (L'Héritier de Nouvelon); 1640: *La Troade* (Sallebray); 1642: *Agamemnon* (Arnaud); 1645: *La Mort de Chrispe* (Tristan); 1646: *Hippolyte* (Gilbert); 1649: *L'Amante Vindicative* (Baro). As a kind of climax to the developing interest in Senecan Theater, Linage published the first *prose* translation into French of Seneca's tragedies in 1651.

In his choice of subject, first of all, Corneille betrays a taste akin to Seneca's. Lancaster says, speaking of *Clitandre:* "Even his liking for the horrible, which recalls Hardy's *Scédase* or *Lucrèce* rather than the plays of Corneille's contemporaries, except Durval and Joyel, indicates a taste that had not changed altogether when he selected Seneca's *Medea* as the subject of his first tragedy." [34] Although the more practical consideration cited above (the success of *Hercule Mourant*) probably weighed more in the choice, Lancaster's point is still well taken.

Revenge is the prime mover in *Medea*, [35] and one of Corneille's additions to the Senecan plot consists in increasing the quantity of vengeance due, by doubling the number of figures seeking reprisal: Médée and Aegée. The whole of Aegée's role and functional importance (probably suggested to Corneille by Euripides' *Medea*) is designed to give breadth to the drama. With this same purpose in mind. Pollux is added as a *confident* of Jason; Créuse actually makes an appearance on stage, and she is given a *confidente*. As Professor Riddle has pointed out, "With personnages added new scenes may be invented, such as those between Jason and Pollux (I, 1), Pollux and Créon (IV, 2 and 3), Aegée and Créuse (II, 5), and Créuse and Jason (II, 4)." [36]

Instead of the traditional opening (Medea alone on stage), Corneille prefers to characterize Jason first, and build up expectation for Médée's arrival in Act I, scene 4. Her long monologue beginning with "Souverains protecteurs des lois de l'hyménée" closely resembles, and in many verses reproduces, Seneca's *Medea*, verses 1-25. [37]

---

[34] Lancaster, part 1, II, 525.

[35] Elliott Forsyth has shown that Seneca's *Medea* and *Thyestes* were two of the major literary sources for the wave of revenge plays within the French classical tradition (see *La Tragédie Française de Jodelle à Corneille*, especially pp. 105-107), and Marvin T. Herrick does the same for Italian dramatic literature in his *Italian Tragedy in the Renaissance* (Urbana, 1965).

[36] Lawrence M. Riddle, *The Genesis and Sources of Pierre Corneille's Tragedies from Médée to Pertharite*, Johns Hopkins Studies in Romance Lit. and Lang., III (Baltimore, 1926), 4. The scenes of Senecan inspiration which Corneille seems to have considered central to the construction of his own *Médée* are: I, 4; II, 2; III, 3; IV, 1; V, 2; and V, 6.

[37] Corneille himself has written (*Théâtre Complet*, Bibliothèque de la Pléiade, Tome I, Paris, 1950, p. 612): "Quant au style, il est fort inégal en

The play moves along at approximately the same pace as the *Medea* (excepting, as has been said, the complications brought on by Aegée), with Médée's lust for vengeance growing and giving expression to an increasing number of threats, until she cries to Jason (III, 3), "Et ce qu'ont fait pour vous mon savoir et ma main / M'a fait un ennemi de tout le genre humain." The point is thereby made that Médée has battled the human race once (for Jason), and the audience well appreciates the intimation that she will do it again — for herself.

In another instance, Médée is made to say, "Et toujours ma fortune a dépendu de moi" (III, 3). These two last quotations adequately display the way in which Corneille frequently strikes the note of self-dependence, or the preservation of self-integrity. As I have indicated, this is the *sine qua non* of Seneca's theater. Corneille uses this theme for several reasons: (1) it is extremely suitable to the nature of the subject; (2) it is a Senecan element, and as Corneille had undoubtedly perceived, Seneca was partially responsible for Rotrou's success, and (3) it is an aspect which contributes admirably to the formation of character as Corneille conceives it.

Finally, in Act III, scene 4, Médée states, "Son faible est découvert" (Seneca: "vulneri patuit locus," verse 550). She puts her plan into effect, and Créon and his daughter are poisoned by the magic cloak. After the slaying of the children, Médée escapes and Jason, in despair, commits suicide. The suicide is Corneille's invention and follows from the character of his Jason, just as it would not follow from the rather pusillanimous Jason of Seneca's creation.

In phraseology, style, and structure, Corneille is obviously indebted to Seneca. However, more significantly, the Cornelian and Senecan conceptions possess substantial similarities which are due to the common interest in the deeds and emotions of a principal figure whose true personality is revealed through conflict. In fact, André Stegmann has recently argued that Corneille discovered the essence of what was to be the Cornelian tragic

---

ce poème; et ce que j'y ai mêlé du mien approche si peu de ce que j'ai traduit de Sénèque, qu'il n'est point besoin d'en mettre le texte en marge pour faire discerner au lecteur ce qui est de lui ou de moi."

dilemma in his adaptation of *Medea:* "Mais l'ultime débat intérieur de Médée, qui ne doit à Sénèque que quelques détails, nous offre autre chose que cette complexe logique sentimentale. Il définit la plénitude de cet étonnement angoissé propre au pathétique cornélien. Corneille en est si conscient que l'apogée de ce crescendo tragique est une véritable définition de la 'situation cornélienne:'

> Je n'exécute rien, et mon âme éperdue
> Entre deux passions demeure suspendue. (1353-1354)

Ainsi, avec la *Médée* de Sénèque, Corneille a découvert non un beau sujet, mais la nature de son propre tragique." [38] We should describe Seneca's influence on Corneille's *Médée*, therefore, as a noteworthy contribution. Later we shall see how central Seneca's presence is to the works of the other great tragic dramatist of the century, Racine.

In a tome entitled, *Le Parnasse ou Le Critique des Poètes* (1635, but anterior to *Hippolyte*), Guérin de La Pinelière writes, in the prefatory *Au Lecteur*, "Je te confesseray librement que je ne me produis que pour me faire conoistre, & pour acquerir de la reputation." It is quite revealing that the young man who wants to make his way literarily — and quickly — should choose Seneca as the model for his first tragedy, *Hippolyte*. In accord with Rotrou and Corneille, La Pinelière could find no classical author more respected or time-tested than Seneca, no one therefore who would present less of a risk for the fledgling tragedian.

In *Hippolyte*, La Pinelière stays quite close to the original Latin, despite his prefatory remarks proclaiming his own creativity. Almost all of the "éloges" addressed to La Pinelière, and printed as *pièces liminaires*, contain references to Seneca, and Benserade's comment is particularly interesting not only because it mentions Seneca, but mainly because behind the direct address to La Pinelière exists a kind of hymn to the renaissance of tragedy:

> Sénèque s'y voyant [in *Hippolyte*] s'est lui mesme admiré
> Et ne s'est pas connu se voyant si paré...

---

[38] "La *Médée* de Corneille," *Les Tragédies de Sénèque et le Théâtre de la Renaissance* (Paris, 1964), p. 125.

Cependant continuë en ces rares merveilles,
Qu'un tragique sujet occupe encore tes veilles,
Maintenant que le peuple en gouste l'entretien
Et qu'on voit de retour le Cothurne Ancien,
Maintenant qu'au plus grave on promet la couronne,
Que la Scene gemit & que la Muse tonne,
Qu'à ce bel Hippolyte un semblable soit joint
Et donne des pareils à ce qui n'en a point,
Glorieux d'estre au front de cette Tragédie
Laisse moy partager l'honneur qu'on te dédie. [39]

The play *Hippolyte* does not have great interest, because it does not contain any noteworthy changes from the Senecan conception, except that the total effect is considerably less powerful. What is remarkable is that, at the moment of new triumph of *tragédie*, another young author looks to the original Seneca for inspiration.

The general trend during the period 1635-1659 is away from the strict imitation of a La Pinelière and toward a more original inventiveness, and thus the Seneca-inspired efforts range from the level of modest imitation to the point where Seneca is barely perceptible amidst the free invention of the French author.

The *Thyeste* (1638) of Monléon is preceded by a preface in which the author pays his respects to Seneca: "Si je t'avois donné cette tragédie de la façon que *Carcinome* ou *Sénèque* l'ont traitée, peut-estre (Lecteur) y aurois-tu trouvé plus d'agreemens [sic], & peut-estre aussi l'aurois-tu estimée trop nuë pour le Theatre d'aujourd'huy."

Monléon does not at all refrain from using Senecan elements; in fact he translates verses 1005-1011 and 1096-1099 of Seneca's *Thyestes* for his own purposes in Act V, scene 5. In addition he closes his play with these words, which are adapted from 1110-1112 of *Thyestes*, "Contant [sic] d'avoir porté ma vengeance à l'extreme, / Je laisse à tes enfans à te punir toy-mesme."

Despite these obvious examples of imitation, Monléon has altered and embellished the original by redistributing the monologues to several characters (instead of letting Atreus and Thyestes speak them all), by creating the roles of Mérope, wife of Atrée, and of several confidants, especially Melinthe, whom Atrée loves.

---

[39] *Hippolyte* (Paris, 1635).

The desire to accord the place of prominence to the love theme is also evident in François de Grenaille's *L'Innocent Malheureux ou La Mort de Chrispe* (1639), which continues the line of "Phèdre" tragedies. Though there are occasional speeches which are Senecan in tone, the differences in conception between Grenaille and Seneca are so considerable that the latter's influence must surely be limited to the very general treatment of the theme.

Phaedra reappears twice more in the period (1635-1659) as a source for French tragedy, in *La Mort de Chrispe* (1644) by Tristan l'Hermite, and also in *Hippolyte* (1646) by Gabriel Gilbert. Both plays are known as "tragédies épurées" within the Phaedra tradition because they evidence a clear attempt to attenuate the shock the legend presents, by not placing the Phaedra figure in any blood relationship to the Hippolytus character. However, the focus remains, as in Seneca, on Phaedra, and several of the techniques recall the Phaedra legend as treated by Seneca and his admirers in France. Gilbert's effort deserves additional notice because, though the Phaedra theme was put to use in later works (*L'Amante Vindicative*, 1649, by Baro, and *Hippolyte*, 1675, by Bidar), Racine apparently chose to borrow a passage from Gilbert for his *Phèdre*. [40]

L'Héritier de Nouvelon's *Hercule Furieux* (1639) contains a curious mélange of elements: within a rhythm that derives basically from Euripides' *Herakles*, there are many direct and important borrowings from Seneca. For example, the very first scene, wherein Mégare soliloquizes, bears a remarkable resemblance to Megara's sentiment in *Hercules Furens* (v. 205-209 and 305-307). Furthermore, the central scenes of Hercules' seizure, then re-awakening, were shaped after a Senecan, not Euripidean, fashion.

The other two tragedies of the period which possess Senecan traces lean more consistently upon invention than does *Hercule Furieux* of L'Heritier de Nouvelon. In Sallebray's *La Troade* (1640)

---

[40] See Frères Parfaict, *Histoire du Théâtre François* (Paris, 1745-1749), VII, 69-71.

the general subject, certain verses, and an occasional scene are reminiscent of Seneca (undoubtedly via Garnier). But these elements are scattered throughout, and the order of events does not follow the Senecan scheme. Arnaud's *Agamemnon* (1642) is also of rather free Senecan inspiration, but the Senecan factors are more easily perceptible: the treatment of the subject (in *most* scenes, not all), the numerous monologues (including an opening soliloquy),[41] the considerable lamentation, and the moment of hesitation before a criminal act. *La Troade* most certainly derives from Seneca's conception, and has little, if anything, to do with Aeschylus.

In general, then, the tragedian of the third and fourth decades of the seventeenth century rarely sought a total conception of a play from Seneca. What he did choose to interpolate into his own work were those specific elements which might enhance the dramatic effectiveness of his presentation. Consequently, a great deal of the best in Seneca's language is borrowed, indeed transposed almost *in toto* into French tragedies. Also, when the seventeenth-century dramatist considered the original treatment by Seneca to be of sufficient worth, he did not destroy the Senecan order, but rather made the Latin plot more concise and full of action. Interestingly, the only two authors, between 1635 and 1660, whose Seneca-inspired dramas possess merit are Tristan and Corneille, which proves once again the sad lesson often repeated in the sixteenth and seventeenth centuries: imitation of a classic is no substitute for talent.

In 1659, Corneille returned to a Senecan subject to launch his "second" career, just as he had originally sought out Seneca for his very first *tragédie:* although *la Toison d'Or* was composed earlier, it was the performance of *Oedipe* that officially hailed Corneille's re-entry into the theatrical world after his self-imposed retirement, and again we should note the resemblance to Seneca.

In the use of subject matter, the debt is not very great: a few passages, the manner of Jocaste's death and Oedipe's inflicting blindness on himself by using his fingernails. Corneille compresses

---

[41] Herein Aegiste reveals what the *spectre* of his father had asked him to do. The actual presentation of the ghost on stage was apparently largely outmoded by this date, if one excepts the "Ombre de Sthénélée" in Gombaud's *Les Danaïdes* of 1646.

into one act almost all the material of Seneca's *Oedipus*, while retaining essentially the same concern to be found in the Senecan opus, namely, self-knowledge and self-integrity.

Throughout the play Oedipe seeks to discover the cause of the plague, and when he learns the truth, he accepts it nobly. The fact that his constant soul-searching has uncovered an ugly crime excites even more admiration for the king than was normally obtained by his regal stature. This "admiration" consists in that awe the spectator feels when confronted with an extreme of conduct, which, by its virtuousness or villany, surpasses the accepted norms (Latin, *admirari*). Horace, Polyeucte and Médée possess this power to inspire admiration perhaps more than the other Cornelian heroes.[42] On this point, René Bray has said: "Mais Corneille est de tous celui qui se libère le plus complètement de la théorie traditionelle des passions tragiques, en joignant ou en substituant au pathétique de la terreur et de la pitié le pathétique de l'admiration."[43] It is unnecessary to recall in detail the major role that admiration plays in Seneca's aesthetic. The figures of Corneille's most important dramas are even more admirable (and perhaps less tragic) than Seneca's in their very uncomplaining acceptance of or victory over the menacing obstacle.

Corneille and Seneca, then, are alike in their taste for the violent in life, and for the clash of interests which stems from the basic desires of individuals. The attention to themes of revenge and ambition is common, not only to the two authors in question,

---

[41A] Despite its title, *La Mort de Sénèque* (1644) of Tristan l'Hermite has nothing specific to do with the Senecan tradition in French Tragedy.

[42] Edith Kern (*The Influence of Heinsius and Vossius on French Dramatic Theory*, Baltimore, 1949), indicates that Vossius exerted no inconsiderable influence on Corneille's dramatic theories. But when Vossius says "admirabile" he means the surprising, amazing, unexpected, whereas for Corneille, it has an ethical sense. Miss Kern then concludes (p. 124): "Now it may be possible that Corneille ... misinterpreted Vossius' *admirabile* and thus arrived at this quite original concept of the effects of tragedy. However, it seems to me that he alone may be credited with its theory as well as its realization." Yet surely Corneille is following Seneca's practice, if not the Roman's announced theory, in creating "admirable" characters: Corneille, like Seneca, was preoccupied with depicting the hero, and one may claim that he perceived Seneca's "admiration" to be especially suited to his own concept of characterization and aesthetic effect.

[43] *La Formation de la Doctrine Classique en France* (Paris, 1927), p. 319.

but also to the lot of French tragedians who were contemporaries of Hardy or immediately succeeded him.

Furthermore, there developed a trend toward the depiction of individuals striving to preserve their self-integrity and what would be more logical than for French dramatists to turn to a time-honored author whose interest in character analysis was of the same nature as theirs, and whose works would consequently be ripe for imitation, adaptation, and as a general source of inspiration? This is what occurred during the resurgence of interest in Seneca which began in the 1630's. [48A]

Mere chance does not explain Corneille's utilization of Seneca as a model for certain of his works, for Senecan drama had much to offer to him in particular. Indeed, because of the theme of self-integrity and the great strength of his characters, Corneille is more Senecan than Rotrou, for example, though the former did much less strict imitation of Seneca. Because of his interest in great heroes and villains whose clashing wills make for dramatic action supported by a powerful, almost overwhelming kind of language, [44] Corneille approaches Seneca more closely than any of the authors already considered. In a sense, the melodramatic in Seneca attracted Corneille — the hyperbolic statements of passion and personal appetite made prominent by contradictory but less intense sentiments of order and balance.

Corneille also occupies a place of prime importance in the Senecan tradition because he appears to have been the first French author to have conceived of his works as drama and not as a literary creation which was, incidentally, to be performed. If Corneille uses Seneca, this must be viewed as a great testimony

---

[48A] Jacques Maurens has devoted a chapter to Seneca's contribution to French humanistic tragedy in his *La Tragédie sans Tragique* (Paris, 1966), pp. 46-66.

[44] Of this language, Raymond Lebègue (*Tragédie Française de la Renaissance*, p. 97) says: "Enfin, les exposés et les discussions d'idées eurent pour résultat d'assouplir et d'enrichir la langue abstraite. Cette forme artistique manquait aux mystères, si l'on met à part quelques morceaux pathétiques ou grandiloquents. Elle manquera à beaucoup de tragédies irrégulières des années 1580-1630. Corneille la portera à la perfection; mais, sur ce point, il ne fera que continuer la voie tracée par Sénèque et par les meilleurs dramaturges du XVIe siècle."

to the possibilities of Senecan theater: not only was Seneca popular with those who wrote from a purely literary point of view, as in the Renaissance, but he retained his prestige when the acid test became his *dramatic* effectiveness.

The presence of Seneca as a dramatic source of inspiration does not cease with Corneille, but continues throughout the rest of the century, as I shall have occasion to indicate. In fact the device of borrowing from or imitating Seneca must have been so well known that Molière selects Seneca as his target in *La Critique de l'Ecole des Femmes* (1663), when he argues that comedy is more difficult to write than tragedy: "... il est bien plus aisé de se guinder sur de grands sentiments, de braver en vers la Fortune, accuser les Destins, et dire des injures aux Dieux, que d'entrer comme il faut dans le ridicule des hommes, et de rendre agréablement sur le théatre les défauts de tout le monde." [45]

There exists, therefore, a Senecan tradition in French serious drama, that is, an unbroken line of plays which draw, more than incidentally, upon Seneca and his disciples. Indeed, he is surely the towering figure among classical models between 1550 and the beginning of Racine's period of creative activity. Af first Senecan theater was considered suitable because of its moral content, enveloped in a rigid form. Then, in the late sixteenth and early seventeenth centuries, as invention replaces imitation, its effect is felt more indirectly than directly, generally through the pervasive influence of Robert Garnier. Finally, after 1632, Seneca's role may be said to be both direct and indirect.

What Racine will inherit generally from this Senecan tradition consists in the late starting point of his tragedies, the observance of the unities, particularly the unity of tone, the clash of passion and politics, and the notion that characters of great magnitude (usually villains) become the most powerful dramatic figures. Perhaps of even broader significance for Racine and his contemporaries who were practicing *tragédie* is the elevated,

---

[45] *Œuvres Complètes de Molière*, Bibliothèque de la Pléiade, I (Paris, 1956), 541. It has been suggested that Corneille should be viewed as Molière's verbal victim here, but this would not seem logical for, as Professor Lancaster has noted, Molière was producing *Cinna* and *Sertorius* at this very time (*French Dramatic Literature*, Part III, I, 255, n. 3).

melodramatic language copied by the Renaissance which becomes an integral part of French classical drama from its inception to its decline in the eighteenth century. The language is considerably purged of excessive Senecan rhetoric, but the basic level of expression of French tragedy derives, originally, from the imitation of Seneca's exalted style.[46]

For these reasons it was not unusual for young dramatists of the early seventeenth century to seek out a Senecan subject for imitation in an attempt to assure an auspicious début to their careers (Rotrou, La Pinelière, Corneille — twice). Curiously, however, no one succeeds either in excelling in the creation of women or in obtaining the incisive effects of Senecan language — achievements which had to await the coming of Racine.

The mere fact that the *Oedipe* of Corneille (inspired, in part, by Seneca) was presented less than five years before Racine's first production *(la Thébaïde,* 1664),[47] coupled with the consideration that Marolles published a prose translation of Seneca's tragedies in 1660 (republished in *1664),* would be sufficient reason for claiming that Senecan theater was influential during the period of Racine's first dramatic efforts. However, the range of tragedies exhibiting Senecan traits which have already been discussed, plus those I will continue to note, leave no doubt as to Seneca's "availability" as a source of inspiration throughout all of the time Racine was writing tragedy.

---

[46] The Renaissance dramatists did not seek their conception of tragic style in their own drama of the Middle Ages, and Greek style is altogether too direct to account for the lofty nature of French tragic verse.

[47] Racine was, of course, thinking of the theater in 1659-60 when he wrote *Amasie*, his first dramatic experiment, which, however, was never performed. Georges May, in *Tragédie Cornélienne, Tragédie Racinienne* (Urbana, 1948), p. 119, notes: "*Oedipe* de Corneille est de 1659; Racine songea au sujet des *Frères* dès 1663; dates et sujets les rapprochent étroitement. Il nous semble infiniment probable que le bruit du succès d'*Oedipe* arriva jusqu'aux oreilles de Racine alors à Paris."

PART THREE
RACINE

CHAPTER I

THEMES: *LA THÉBAÏDE*

Jean Racine's choice of *La Thébaïde* as the subject of his first publicly produced play fits in well with the impression one has of the young Racine. Desiring to launch a dramatic career, he selects a memorable adventure from ancient legend, copies much of Rotrou's version of the story, and — as Rotrou, Corneille, and others had done before him — adds a measure of Seneca to the mixture in an effort to assure success.

In the preface to *La Thébaïde ou Les Frères Ennemis* Racine states: "Car pour *la Thébaïde* qui est dans Sénèque, je suis un peu de l'opinion d'Heinsius, et je tiens, comme lui, que non seulement ce n'est point une tragédie de Sénèque, mais que c'est plutot l'ouvrage d'un déclamateur, qui ne savait ce que c'etait que tragédie." [1]

---

[1] Jean Racine, *Œuvres,* ed. Paul Mesnard (Paris: Hachette, 1910-1912), I, 404. (All subsequent quotations will be taken from this edition.) The quotation cited above proves in a concrete manner that Racine had read Seneca's tragedies, undoubtedly in the edition published with Heinsius' critical annotations at Leyden in 1611. An examination of the contents of Racine's library discloses that he had a copy of Seneca's philosophical works, and later on in life he acquired a copy of the tragedies. (See P. Bonnefon, "La Bibliothèque de Racine," *Revue d'Histoire Littéraire,* V [1898], 169-219.) On page 213 Bonnefon lists the following works as having belonged to Racine's library: *L. Annaei Senecae philosophi omnia opera.* Ludg. Batav. apud Elzeviros. 1649, 4 vol. in-12; *L. et M. Annaei Senecae Tragoediae, cum notis Farnabii.* Amstelodami, apud Dan. Elzevier. 1678, in-24. However, Racine undoubtedly encountered the tragedies for the first time during his early training in the classics.

This declaration is of capital importance for several reasons: it contains the first mention of Seneca among Racine's dramatic writings, and its statement that the *Phoenissae* is not worthy of true Seneca betrays Racine's respect for Senecan drama. It also constitutes the first example of the manner in which Racine will consciously avoid admitting his debt to Seneca. Yet, however poor his opinion of the *Phoenissae*, he evidently employed parts of it in composing his own play. (We should keep in mind the fact that the preface to *La Thébaïde* was composed for the 1676 edition of the collected works. And so this "first" pronouncement on Seneca must be interpreted in the light of Racine's position and mentality, not as a neophyte, but as the acknowledged master of French tragedy, some short time before the presentation of *Phèdre*.)

Unlike Rotrou's *Antigone*, whose Senecan traits are found only in the first two acts, Racine's *La Thébaïde* exhibits such traits throughout. The subject matter of the Racinian drama is derived in great part from Rotrou, as are many of the verses which recall Seneca. But the direct imitation of Seneca also plays a part, as in the many verses closely parallel to the Senecan text.

Racine's first full play relies for its basic material upon the well-received works of predecessors. This is typical not only of the authors of the seventeenth century, but of French *littérateurs* in general. French literature is much more "literary," more conscious of and indebted to the works of previous ages for its inspiration than English literature, for example, and consequently the weight of tradition is felt more acutely by the French author than by his English counterpart.

Certainly one can see apparent traces of Euripides[2] as well as of Rotrou in *La Thébaïde*. But, the most striking analogy between Seneca and Racine that one can find in *La Thébaïde* lies in the category of themes, and this play will serve admirably

---

[2] P. Mesnard (Racine, *Œuvres*, I, 386) notes first of all "beaucoup de traits heureux, et vraiment tragiques, fournis par Sénèque." He adds, later on the same page: "Quant à Euripide, les quelques vers de ses *Phéniciennes* qu'on peut rapprocher des vers de *la Thébaïde* avaient déjà, à peu d'exceptions près, été imités par Sénèque ou par Rotrou, et on est en droit de douter que notre auteur les ait toujours pris à la premiere source...."

as a *point de départ* for a comparison of Senecan and Racinian thematic usage.

Act I of *La Thébaïde* contains expository matter which is quite close in spirit to the opening lines of the second fragment of the *Phoenissae,* wherein the preparation for the Polyneices — Eteocles confrontation is laid. In fact, Seneca-inspired lines are found in important passages in the first act: verses 17 and 18 of Racine are close in meaning and rhythm to 407-409 of Seneca; there exists the possible rapport between verses 23-24 and *Phaedra,* 677-680. Créon enters in scene 4 and immediately begins to sow that hatred and dissension whose effects form the heart of the tragedy. There was no Créon in the *Phoenissae,* but Rotrou had inserted him and Racine makes effective, if exaggerated, use of him as the catalyst for all the destruction which will be unleashed. Créon is also the figure who will upset the apparent balance of the characters: Polynice-Étéocle, Antigone Hémon, Jocaste-Créon. Créon breaks through and into the other relationships with tragic effect. [3]

At the end of the first act, therefore, the seeds of the principal themes have been sown: discord in all its forms (exile, political strife, hatred between the closest of kin, the unnatural desire of the older man [Créon] for his niece Antigone), and the love of Antigone for Hémon. All but the last two are also to be found in the *Phoenissae,* even in its abbreviated form. Moreover, though themes of passion are not sewn into the fabric of the *Phoenissae,* one must remember that they are not at all foreign to Senecan drama. Indeed, as has been pointed out in an earlier chapter, Seneca, among the ancients, displays the greatest literary preoccupation with passion and its effects.

Acts II and III are conditioned by the exigencies of several subplots which Racine chooses to include, and consequently have no resemblance to any events in Seneca's play. Act II concerns

---

[3] Georges Poulet in his *Études sur le Temps Humain* (Paris, 1949), also sees Créon as the principal figure, despite the apparent direction given the play by its title (p. 105): "Quel est le sujet de *la Thébaïde?* C'est l'histoire d'un homme qui croit pouvoir s'affranchir du passé.... Créon seul rêve d'un état où, dans l'actualité absolue que confère la toute-puissance il soit possible de s'affranchir d'un coup de cette fatale fidélité."

the love, expressed in most courtly terms, of Hémon for Antigone, and the attempt to bend the inflexible Polynice. The report of a treacherous attack on Polynice's forces during a period of truce terminates the act and all immediate hope of reconciliation.

Act III reveals the self-sacrifice of Ménécée and the blunt confession of regal ambition by Créon. In this act the play turns its focus firmly upon Créon and his importance will grow until he clearly emerges as the main character.

In Act IV the thread of Seneca's *Phoenissae* shows through once more in evident similarities of verse structure. This is to be expected, since Racine's fourth act centers about the Étéocle-Polynice confrontation, which forms the moment of greatest intensity of the second fragment of the Senecan play. Indeed, scene 3, which comprises 80 per cent of the fourth act of *La Thébaïde*, draws its inspiration almost exclusively from the *Phoenissae*, and in many instances follows closely both the spirit and the letter of the Senecan text.

In the midst of their quarrel the spectator sees the brothers for the last time in Seneca. The fragment ends with the sententious exclamation of Eteocles, "Imperia pretio quolibet constant bene" ["Sovereignty is well bought at any price"]. Therefore the Senecan text could not have aided Recine in completing his play in the fifth act. If Racine consulted an author for details for his denouement it is Statius, but in general the last act is of Racine's own creation. In it are related the deaths of Polynice, Étéocle, Jocaste, Hémon, and Antigone, and it is then that Créon uncovers his plans and desires, only to be finally frustrated.[4]

As we have seen, Seneca's tragedies revolve about crimes and their responsibility, and both are influenced by the deeds of the characters' forebears. In particular, *Thyestes* and *Agamemnon* concern revenge exacted for hereditary guilt. Heredity is a form of curse upon the descendants of a family, and the working out of this curse governs the actions of the people involved. Indeed, so horrible will be the act committed in *Agamemnon* (the massacre of the title character) that Thyestes' ghost, who

---

[4] Créon's cry (1494), "Ah! c'est m'assassiner que me sauver la vie," seems to imitate *Phoenissae* (100), "Occidere est, vetare cupientem mori." ["'Tis the same as killing to forbid death to him who wants it."]

appears in the prologue, trembles at the thought of it. Moreover, the very use of ghosts who are ancestors of the characters in the play betrays Seneca's Stoic preoccupation with heredity as a force (like passion) capable of exerting a nefarious influence on man's reason.

In *La Thébaïde*, Racine takes up this very same theme, particularly as it had been put to use in the *Phoenissae*. For Racine it is a way of demonstrating the past's imposition on the present. Every major character in *La Thébaïde* succumbs to the curse on the House of Laius which realizes its destructive potential on the day appointed for the Étéocle-Polynice confrontation. In *Britannicus* Racine poses this dramatic question: when will Néron divest himself of "trois ans de vertu" and show himself to be the true descendant of the ruthless Roman emperors? *Phèdre* too reveals this force of the past. The queen herself discloses her painful awareness of "la haine de Vénus" and the ills it has worked upon her family. The struggle which takes place within Phèdre can thus be viewed as her vain attempt to disengage herself totally from a past which shows all signs of giving direction to her present conduct.

Athalie presents an aspect of the same theme, which is unusual, however, in that the curse is cast forward into the future at the end of the play. (Ordinarily the present result of a past act is portrayed.) In her last speech Athalie cries out her hopes that Joas will turn upon his God and avenge her. In so doing he will be (1786-1787), "Fidèle au sang d'Achab, qu'il a reçu de moi, / Conforme à son aïeul, à son père semblable...." And finally, after calling him "de David *l'héritier* détestable" [italics mine], she leaves the stage.

Racine resembles Seneca in his application of the possibilities of the theme of heredity to tragedy. However, whereas Seneca's goal lies in strengthening the motive for vengeance, and in pursuing an almost clinical examination of hereditary effect on the normally rational conduct of man, Racine sees the advantage of the theme in giving nuance to a central problem: guilt and human responsibility. *Phèdre* remains the prime example.

Furthermore, the past weighs heavily upon Racine's characters, and heredity is a concrete way of symbolizing all that has already happened which will serve to create the crisis that is to take place in the appointed twenty-four hours, the end of the journey for Racine's characters. Heredity in Racine, then, is the most skilful tool of fate.

The second theme of importance is that of politics. In *La Thébaïde*, as in the rest of Racine's plays, the tragic situation evolves within a political context.[5] The application of this theme in both Racine and Seneca has interesting results. Besides the obvious interest generated by a clash of wills at the highest level, and for the greatest of material gains, the use of politics affords a means of focusing the action in the present. Because the throne becomes the prize at stake usually *during* the course of the play, and because a decision as to possession has to be made then and there, a sense of immediacy is imparted to the play. Whatever else may happen, the political situation must be resolved, at least temporarily, before the play ends. And so there is a concentration upon events as they happen, and not on what has occurred or will happen.

Both Racine and Seneca have recourse to politics as an instrument of depiction of character memorably in the case of Phèdre, and her Latin model, Phaedra. The heroine offers to yield this most cherished of all material possessions, if it will aid in securing the affection of the beloved. In the context of these plays this willingness to surrender the throne is highly effective in indicating a system of values, for the heroine refuses what has been sought by so many others: power.

However, if one considers the Racinian and Senecan repertories *in toto*, a distinction must be made here. For Seneca, and undoubtedly for his contemporaries, political strength was an ultimate goal, and the uses of it were of vast interest, as is evidenced by the many discussions of the problem that are scattered throughout the Senecan corpus. Racine prefers to deploy his political themes as means to an end: when forced to choose between possession of the realm and the possible possession of the beloved, the Racinian character makes a rapid and unalterable

---

[5] Although the political theme of the rights and obligations of imperial power so dear to Seneca is touched upon briefly in *La Thébaïde*, it finds its fullest Racinian expression in *Britannicus* and *Bérénice*.

choice of the second alternative, in direct contrast to what is seen in both Seneca and in the major plays of Corneille. Thus Racine allows but meager time to the controversy over the best political systems, for his interest is elsewhere.

Another major theme is that of captivity and exile. All of the exiles in Seneca serve the reasonable dramatic purpose of inducing a favorable sentimental reaction. The characters who are captives have this function, but they also demonstrate the suffering Seneca saw as necessarily attached to the human condition.

Exile as a theme runs through the majority of Racine's repertory. In *La Thébaïde,* his very first play, he establishes Polynice's exile as the result of the legendary hatred between the "*frères ennemis,*" and it serves two purposes: political advantage (for Étéocle), and, more significantly, physical separation. Born of incest, Étéocle and Polynice show a fundamental aversion to personal contact with each other (933: "Plus il approche, et plus il me semble odieux"). The irony lies in the continued efforts by other characters, especially Jocaste, to bring them together. Once contact is made, mutual destruction ensues. Thus, Polynice's exile is only temporarily effective in avoiding the inevitable. [6]

The working out of the theme in *Andromaque* takes on a more complex air. Andromaque, a Trojan in Epirus, is both an exile and a captive on the physical level alone. But beyond that, she has resolved to carry on as an exile; indeed her existence seems to revolve around this state, for, even though a stranger in Epirus, she asks for a further exile (338), "Seigneur, c'est un exil que mes pleurs vous demandent." Moreover, her condition

---

[6] A variant gives a precious clue to the first use of exile as a reflection of profounder estrangement — from oneself. Polynice exclaims (variant to verses 1054 ff.):

Je ne me connais plus en ce malheur extrême:
En m'arrachant au trône on m'arrache à moi-même.
Tant que j'en suis dehors, je ne suis plus à moi.

In fact Créon and Jocaste make similar statements of self-alienation. Créon (1459-1460): "Tout ce qui s'est passé n'est qu'un songe pour moi: : J'étais père et sujet, je suis amant et roi." Jocaste (1188-1189): "Je n'ai plus pour mon sang ni pitié ni tendresse: / Votre exemple m'apprend à ne le plus chérir."

as prisoner and foreigner renders her hope for success all the more distant and her own position extremely sympathetic.

Oreste arrives in Epirus, a foreign land, after a long voyage. He confesses that he is a captive of sorts — of his love for Hermione, and that he has travelled far and wide in his quest. Yet he must admit that it is really death which has attracted but constantly avoided him (496), "A chercher dans vos yeux une mort qui me fuit." At last, however, he is condemned to wander forever, physically alive, mentally dead.

Hermione too, it must be remembered, is a stranger in Epirus, and more than that, she is basically a captive, for she is bound by honor to remain in the foreign land with her fiancé, but more intensely is she a prisoner of her own passion for Pyrrhus. And so Hermione lives as an outsider, suspended in Epirus between her inclination for Pyrrhus, and her pride which urges her to leave before being humiliated. As the drama nears its close, Hermione makes her choice: exile and alienation from all she used to hold dear rather than repatriation (1561-1563):

> ...Je demeure en Epire:
> Je renonce à la Grèce, à Sparte, à son empire,
> A toute ma famille....

To continue this listing, one can turn to *Britannicus* and find another captive, Junie. *Bérénice* contains two foreigners (Bérénice and Antiochus), and at the end both leave for their own countries, considered, paradoxically, as places of exile. Moreover, Titus describes his own state in these words (751-754):

> Ah! Prince, jurez-lui que toujours trop fidèle,
> Gémissant dans ma cour, et plus exilé qu'elle,
> Portant jusqu'au tombeau le nom de son amant,
> Mon règne ne sera qu'un long banissement.

In *Bajazet* the title character is a prisoner literally, but how much more of a captive (of her own passion) is Roxane. A captive princess, Monime, possesses the principal female role in *Mithridate*. *Iphigénie* presents to us Eriphile, who states (470), "C'est peu d'être étrangère, inconnue et captive," but whose difficulties arise precisely from her condition as "étrangère, inconnue et captive." *Esther* concerns a woman who is a foreigner to Persia and her fellow Jews, who are treated as outsiders and prospective captives. In *Athalie* Mathan is an outsider, and Athalie has made herself, in effect, a foreigner to her own people, the Jews.

Exile and captivity play significant roles in *Phèdre*. Aricie is a captive; Thésée seems to be in a state of continuous wandering — a sort of self-willed exile. Théramène and Hippolyte explain that they have voyaged widely, and in fact, Hippolyte was exiled from Athens by Phèdre at one time. But the exile of major interest is Phèdre herself. The fact that she lives in a foreign land is the symbol of a greater estrangement. Phèdre is a captive of her own self-knowledge, and because she knows herself she realizes that she is the universal exile: an outsider to the world because she has defiled it with her illegitimate desires. Yet she is a prisoner with no means of escape or concealment, and thus her plight is desperate and particularly *pathétique*.

Unlike Seneca, then, whose major (and at times sole) object in portraying exiles consists in gaining the audience's support for the stranger, Racine wishes to make of physical displacement the symbol of emotional estrangement, for surely what most Racinian characters seek — and fail to find — is a reciprocated love. (And even those innocent characters who can unite in love are crushed by others' selfish desire — that is, misdirected love.) Because of their lack of success, Racine's major figures will continue to wander, never to know the satisfaction of possession and peace of soul.

And so there is a kind of projection into the future where certain characters will never reach the port, but will be constant voyagers, since their fate is to lead the existence of an exile. Through the themes of heredity, politics, and exile, therefore, Racine is able to furnish us with the totality of existence of the inhabitants of his tragic universe: their past, which weighs upon them so heavily, their anguished present, and their hopeless future.

Finally, there exists a more profound thematic rapport between Racine and Seneca which first sees the literary light of day in *La Thébaïde:* the reversal of the laws of nature as a source of tragic irony. Closely allied with the notion of heredity, this aspect gives new dimension to the fratricidal struggle. Just as Seneca's

Jocasta knows that the brothers' conflict is unnatural,[7] so Racine's Étéocle is conscious of the situation, and the fact that one of the brothers expresses it makes the Racinian image all the sharper (919-924):

> Nous étions ennemis dès la plus tendre enfance;
> Que dis-je? nous l'étions avant notre naissance.
> Triste et fatal effet d'un sang incestueux!
> Pendant qu'un même sein nous renfermoit tous deux,
> Dans les flancs de ma mère une guerre intestine
> De nos divisions lui marqua l'origine.

This theme appears again in the semi-fratricidal conflict of Néron and Britannicus in *Britannicus*, and, more profoundly, in the dire strife that separates the two predatory creatures who are the play's principal characters, Agrippine and her son Néron. In addition, there is a reversal or retrogression of a sort in Néron's evolution from "trois ans de vertu" to the historical Nero, madman and murderer. This aspect is given particular emphasis through one of the many antitheses which fill the first act (28-34):

> *Albine:* Il la gouverne en père. Enfin Néron naissant
> A toutes les vertus d'Auguste vieillissant.
> *Agrippine:* Non, non, mon intérêt ne me rend point injuste:
> Il commence, il est vrai, par où finit Auguste;
> Mais crains que l'avenir détruisant le passé,
> Il ne finisse ainsi qu'Auguste a commencé.

The first two verses were probably inspired by a similar though stronger comment by Seneca in the *De Clementia* (Book I, chapter XI), "Comparare nemo mansuetudini tuae audebit divum Augustum, etiam si in certamen iuvenilium annorum deduxerit senectutem plus quam maturam" ["To compare the mildness of the deified Augustus with yours no one will dare, even if the years of youth shall be brought into competition with an old age that

---

[7] Cf. *Phoenissae*, 451-454.

was more than ripe."][8] Racine twists Seneca's statement to introduce the idea of Néron's unusual capacity for evil.[9]

Seneca employs this theme frequently, and to varying degrees, throughout his repertory: with an incestuous basis in *Oedipus* and *Phaedra,* as the unnatural hatred of a wife for her husband *(Agamemnon)* plus the slaying of her own children *(Medea),* and as the reason for attacking another member of one's own family *(Phoenissae, Thyestes).* John Lapp has noted this Senecan theme in Racine, and makes this comment: "L'ironie tragique due au renversement de l'ordre naturel me paraît sénéquienne plutôt qu'euripidienne; elle se reflète clairement dans les tragédies de Racine, surtout *Britannicus,* où Agrippine fait appel aux sentiments filiaux de Néron, *Mithridate,* et *Phèdre.*"[10]

I think it imposible to say whether Racine drew this vital part of his dramatic conception from Seneca, or whether he chose *La Thébaïde* and *Britannicus* as subjects because they would afford him the opportunity for exploiting the possibilities of a theme of his own conception which had a reflection in a basically Senecan situation. In either event, the Racine-Seneca affinity on this point is undeniable.

Finally, in adding a love plot to *La Thébaïde* Racine is following the dictates of French classical tragedy. Although this theme is not well developed, there does appear to exist in Créon an element of that destructive species of selfish passion which will become an integral part of Racine's theater with *Andromaque.*[11]

---

[8] Translation by John Basore from *Seneca's Moral Essays* (New York: G. P. Putnam's Sons, 1928).

[9] In his "Racine est-il Sénéquien?" (*Les Tragédies de Sénèque et le Théâtre de la Renaissance* [Paris, 1964]), John Lapp propounds an interesting theory (p. 132): "Pourtant nous nous souvenons moins souvent que ce traité [*De Clementia*] était adressé à Néron, et que si l'auteur y parle de la clémence d'Auguste c'est uniquement pour faire valoir celle de son maître. Racine, avec son sens très aigu de l'histoire, aurait-il manqué de remarquer que la date du traité de Sénèque coïncidait avec celle du meurtre de Britannicus, et que la louange de Néron qui se trouve dans le *De la Clémence* était donc un exemple d'une ironie créée par l'histoire, de 'l'avenir détruisant le passé?' "

[10] *Ibid.,* p. 131.

[11] As seen in Créon, this passion assumes the form of an impossible desire to possess — really to incorporate into one's being — a totally foreign

All the themes we have cited are indispensable components of both Racinian and Senecan drama. But Racine skilfully turns what may have been Senecan themes to his own particular ends, emphasizing the passionate while de-emphasizing the political, tracing almost clinically the effects of heredity on his creations, drawing the fullest meaning out of the theme of exile, and displaying the unnatural discord that underlies his view of the universe.

---

element: innocence. This seems to be Antigone's great attractiveness for him, and it suggests why Créon's conception of Antigone's death is couched in terms of her eyes closing — as if the light (and purity) of his world had been extinguished (1480-1482):

> Et vous-même, cruelle, éteignez vos beaux yeux!
> Vous fermez pour jamais ces beaux yeux que j'adore;
> Et, pour ne me point voir, vous les fermez encore!

Chapter II

CHARACTERS: *ANDROMAQUE*

In his *Première Préface* to *Andromaque* Racine again has occasion to mention Seneca, as he explains: "Toute la liberté que j'ai prise, ç'a été d'adoucir un peu la férocité de Pyrrhus, que Sénèque, dans sa *Troade*, et Virgile dans le second [sic] de l'*Énéide*, ont poussée beaucoup plus loin que je n'ai cru le devoir faire."

Pyrrhus and Andromaque are the only characters who carry over from Seneca to Racine. Furthermore the two plays (the *Troades* and *Andromaque*) lead to two very different conclusions: the former ends with Andromacha humiliated and crushed, and Astyanax slain; in the latter, Andromaque emerges triumphant over her enemies and saves her son, at least temporarily. Where then does the similarity lie? Basically in character delineation. And so, we can put *Andromaque* to good use as a model for the way in which Racinian and Senecan conceptions of character often run parallel.

Even if Seneca does not lend his presence in an important way to the denouement of *Andromaque*, his spirit seems to haunt the psychological preparation of the crisis: one can make no *rapprochements* of verse or situation between the Senecan and Racinian texts after Act IV, scene 5 of *Andromaque*.[1] Racine

---

[1] R. C. Knight (*Racine et la Grèce*, Paris, 1950, p. 284) has noted that there are echoes of several poets, including Seneca (*Medea, Hercules Oetaeus*) in the scene of Oreste's madness, but the contribution of Seneca is negligible in comparison with that of Euripides.

apparently draws upon Seneca and Seneca-inspired Rotrou [2] for his preparatory acts and then brings the drama to its zenith of interest and emotion through his own invention, with perhaps some aid from Virgil and Euripides. Seneca's presence is principally felt, therefore, in laying the foundation of the tragedy.

The very first words of Oreste to Pyrrhus, at the beginning of the second scene of Act I (verse 143), are an almost exact literal translation of verses 526 and 527 of the *Troades,* where Ulysses says to Andromacha, "Graiorum omnium / procerumque vox est..." ["It is the voice of all the Grecian chiefs...."]. Oreste, in Racine, is made to say, "Avant que tous les Grecs vous parlent par ma voix.'" This borrowing by Racine is not indiscriminate: it is central to the play's action that Oreste officially represents the Greeks and has their support.

The rest of this scene involves the present state of Troy in ruins and the Greeks' concern over the possible future revenge exacted by Astyanax, [3] including Pyrrhus' mordant comment (179-180), "Qu'un peuple tout entier, tant de fois triomphant, / N'eût daigné conspirer que la mort d'un enfant?" This finds its source in the *Troades,* verses 754-755, where Andromacha lashes out at Ulysses, with "Hoc est pectoris facinus tui. / nocturne miles, fortis in pueri necem" [This is the deed of thine own heart. Thou nocturnal soldier, brave to do a mere boy to death...."].

Pyrrhus' confession of guilt for his excessive blood-letting in the battle for Troy reveals a new facet of the otherwise stern son of Achilles. Racine brings out Pyrrhus' guilty conscience by means of another obvious reminiscence from Seneca, made clear by a comparison of the two texts:

    ... fateor, aliquando impotens
    regno ac superbus altius memet tuli;

---

[2] Gustave Rudler has carefully demonstrated *Andromaque*'s debt to Rotrou's *Hercule Mourant.* However, as regards characterization, it seems clear to me that Andromaque has much more in common with the finely executed Andromacha of Seneca than with the unconvincing Iole of Rotrou's creation. See Rudler, "Une Source d'*Andromaque*," *Modern Language Review,* XII (1917), 286-301, 438-449.

[3] Racine 143 = Seneca 527 and 528; R. 158-161 = S. 530-534, 551-552; R. 201-204 = S. 3-7, 740-742; R. 217-220 = S. 286-288. And in the same act: R. 333-334 = S. 471-477; R. 376-377 = S. 409-422.

>   sed regi frenis nequit
> et ira et ardens hostis et victoria
> commissa nocti. quidquid indignum aut ferum
> cuiquam videri potuit, hoc fecit dolor
> tenebraeque, per quas ipse se irritat furor,
> gladiusque felix, cujus infecti semel
> vecors libido est. (*Troades*, 266 and 267, 279-285)

["In the past, I grant, I have been headstrong in government and borne myself too haughtily; ... But wrath, the fiery foeman, victory given to night's charge, these cannot be kept in hand. All that any might have deemed unworthy in me or brutal, this resentment wrought and darkness, whereby fury is spurred to greater fury, and the victorious sword, whose blood-lust, when once stained with blood, is madness."]

> La victoire et la nuit, plus cruelle que nous,
> Nous excitoient au meurtre, et confondoient nos coups.
> Mon courroux aux vaincus ne fut que trop sévère. (211-213)

The main Senecan elements reappear in the Racinian text, though in a concise form: the darkness inciting the victors to bloodshed, the desire for complete (indeed excessive) domination and destruction, the avowal of a hatred that surpassed the limits of reason. To make some sort of atonement (which would transform him into another Hector in Andromaque's eyes), Pyrrhus then admits that "L'Épire sauvera ce que Troie a sauvé," which constitutes another Senecan borrowing.[4]

In scene 4 of this same first act Andromaque appears, and Pyrrhus begins to discuss Astyanax, whom he hopes to use in a game of amorous blackmail: either Andromaque submits and becomes his queen, or the boy is delivered to the Greeks, who still fear the son of Hector. "Digne objet de leur crainte," remarks Andromaque sarcastically (270), and yet pathetically, just as her counterpart in the *Troades* had exclaimed to Ulysses (707-708), "Hic est, hic est terror, Vlixe / mille carinis" ["Here he is, Ulysses, here is the terror of a thousand ships!"].

At the very end of Act I, Andromaque claims that, once Astyanax is dead, she will follow him, since she has no further

---

[4] Cf. 285-286 of the *Troades*, "quicquid eversae potest / superesse Trojae maneat." ["All that can survive of ruined Troy let it survive."]

excuse for living.[5] For this reason Pyrrhus weakens and permits her to see her son. Here again Seneca's *Troades* furnishes a parallel, and a rather close one (418-420):

> iam erepta Danais coniugem sequerer meum,
> nisi hic teneret: hic meos animos domat
> morique prohibet.

["And now, escaping the Greeks, I should follow my husband, if this child held me not. He tames my spirit and prevents my death."]

Racine, then, in creating his character Andromaque, made her express sentiments which disclose her pride and resolution but also her tenderness and maternal affection. These are precisely the qualities which appear in the Latin Andromacha. The resemblance is remarkable and undoubtedly was desired by Racine, for, as I have noted earlier, Seneca's women are marvelous creations, dramatically capable of a broad range of emotions, and Andromacha ranks among the very best, along with Medea and Phaedra.

One discerns in both the Senecan and Racinian Andromaches the same anguish, born of passion and respect for the deceased Hector on the one hand, and a natural affection for her child, which, as the circumstances have it, lies in opposition to her love for the dead hero. The moments of indecision, then, are supreme and give rise to that suspense which underlines all good drama. Indeed, the human side of many of Racine's characters shows through at precisely such times, whether it be Andromaque, Phèdre, Athalie, or Néron. Donald Clive Stuart has made this observation: "His [Racine's] hero vacillates between the two courses open to him.... Racine's characters have some of Hamlet's indecision which causes suspense and enables the playwright to show both sides of the situation."[6] Of course, in Racine the indecision exists on only the human, and therefore illusory level, for the tragic sentiment defines that the hero should have no

---

[5] Verses 376-377, "Sa mort avancera la fin de mes ennuis. / Je prolongeois pour lui ma vie et ma misère."

[6] *The Development of Dramatic Art* (New York, 1928), p. 409.

real choice, but is destined to one course of action. The character, however, does make a decision he considers his own, and it is irrevocable, to his great sorrow. The example which always comes to mind is that of Thésée and his curse upon Hippolyte.

This hesitation just considered should be added to the list of techniques which Racine and Seneca share. Although employed without appreciable skill in most instances (except that of Andromacha), personal indecision and wavering serve as means for Seneca's revelation of character. It is the moment of pause (alas! all too brief) in the character's headlong rush to grasp the object of highest value to him. Racine uses this device with more subtlety to intensify the dilemma and resultant torment of his creations.

The monologue which usually contains the moments of vacillation occurs with relative frequency in French drama. Jacques Scherer has termed it the "monologue à hésitations," and describes it thus: "Un premier type de monologues présentera une succession de réactions affectives, de pensées, de résolutions éphémères, qui se détruisent les unes les autres. Grâce à lui, la psychologie du personnage pourra être mieux étudiée et des articulations pourront se dessiner dans une tirade qui imitera le mouvement de la vie."[7] Perhaps the "monologue à hésitations" is a Senecan legacy to French classical tragedy of the sixteenth and seventeenth centuries.

Act II presents Hermione for the first time. The cycle of tormented lovers is complete: Oreste and Hermione; Hermione and Pyrrhus; Pyrrhus and Andromaque; and, in a sense, Andromaque and Hector. Even in such a general scheme one can easily see the tragic situation, for the passion passes from left to right, so to speak, and never from right to left. Or if a circular motion is more expressive, then the affection moves clockwise, but at no time in the opposite direction.

However, because of the "huis clos" nature of the Racinian universe (a universe first completely defined in *Andromaque*), every action has a double effect. When Hermione shows her preference for Pyrrhus, she also implicitly betrays her rejection

---

[7] *La Dramaturgie Classique*, p. 248.

of Oreste. The same holds true for Pyrrhus with Hermione and Andromaque, Andromaque with Pyrrhus and Hector, and Oreste with his duty and Hermione.

There is an even further refinement: Racine permits his characters to express their frustrated love through hatred. Consequently, Hermione can say with passionate logic (416), "Ah! — je l'ai trop aimé pour ne le point haïr." The verse quoted is of double importance in that it throws into relief the kind of passion which forms the core of the drama, and it is, in addition, another possible Senecan reminiscence. In *Medea* the main figure urges herself on in these words (397-398), "Si quaeris odio, misera, quem statues modum: / imitare amorem" ["If thou seekst, poor soul, what limit thou shouldst set to hate, copy thy love."]. One would expect that the *Troades* alone would be Racine's point of interest when composing *Andromaque*, but one encounters here and in at least one other place [8] indications which point toward *Medea*. And so, on the basis of *Andromaque* alone, one could assume Racine's thorough knowledge of Seneca's plays.

From a consideration of all the verses in *Andromaque* for which one could cite Senecan counterparts, it becomes apparent, first of all, that Racine leans heavily upon Seneca for his portrayal of Andromaque. Moreover, Racine chooses those Senecan lines which portray an Andromacha running the gamut of emotions: torment, maternal affection, a sentiment of honor and self-esteem, despair, self-sacrifice. The wise selection of these lines in itself points to the master craftsman, but Racine progresses beyond this, and populates his Andromaque's world with creatures equally tormented, who seem to exist only to torture one another, in spite of themselves. This concept of a universe of multiple personal tragedy is generally foreign to Seneca, although it does exist in *Phaedra*, where both the title character and Theseus are tragic figures. There is also an attempt at something of this nature in the *Troades*, in which both Hecuba and Andromacha undergo extreme suffering.

---

[8] Act IV, scene 5.

The performance of Pyrrhus in the scene of confrontation with Hermione (IV, 5)[9] typifies his conduct whenever Andromaque is not present. He gives the impression of being the true son of Achilles — hard, unflinching, even heartless (with regard to Hermione). Yet the "captor becomes a captive" in Andromaque's presence, or indeed even when she may be absent but is occupying his mind. Passion, inflamed by the sight of the beloved, remains for a certain time as master after the disappearance of the physical source of the love. Such is the basis for the almost pathetic words of Pyrrhus in Act II (625-626), "Hé bien, Phoenix, l'amour est-il le maître? / Tes yeux refusent-ils encor de me connaître?"

What is of interest in the make-up of this character is precisely that Pyrrhus, the bold, confident soldier has a direct counterpart in Seneca's Pyrrhus from the *Troades*. Seneca does extend his portrayal, so that his character shows not only a certain sternness, but also a ruthlessness and vicious impetuosity which Racine does not choose to infuse into his Pyrrhus.

Instead, Racine prefers to create a more complex Pyrrhus, who would be in keeping with the expectations of the French audience of 1667. However, several of the key Racinian passages which serve to reduce Pyrrhus' stature somewhat, and therefore to make him more human and susceptible to strong passion, have echoes in Seneca. The rejected Hermione remarks (1333-1336):

> Du vieux père d'Hector la valeur abattue
> Aux pieds de sa famille expirante à sa vue,
> Tandis que dans son sein votre bras enfoncé
> Cherche un reste de sang que l'âge avoit glacé.

---

[9] This particular scene greatly resembles the confrontation of Medea and Jason (431-559) in Seneca's *Medea*. Medea, like Hermione, is rebuffed and takes a firm resolution as to the means of her most cruel of vengeances. What follows in both plays is the direct outcome of these scenes, and their importance is to be weighed thereby. (Auguste Widal has also noticed this. See p. 149 of his *Etudes sur trois tragédies de Sénèque*, Paris, 1854.) In "Les Préjugés les plus pernicieux à l'égard de la Littérature Latine" (*Bulletin de l'Association Guillaume Budé*, octobre, 1964, 326-341) Ettore Paratore suggests (p. 339) a parallel between the elegiac tone of Hermione's complaints and that of Dejanira in *Hercules Oetaeus*.

And Hecuba likewise recalls (*Troades,* 46-50):

> ... cum ferox, scaeva manu
> coma reflectens regium torta caput,
> alto nefandum vulneri ferrum abdidit;
> quod penitus actum cum recepisset libens,
> ensis senili siccus e iugulo redit.
> ["When he, with left hand clutching the old man's hair, bent back the royal head and into the deep wound savagely thrust the impious steel; and when with right good will he had plucked away the deep-driven sword, it came unwetted from the old man's throat."]

Again, Oreste's derogatory comparison of Pyrrhus with his father Achilles (148), "Hector tomba sous lui, Troie expira sous vous," has its model in Agamemnon's (235-236), "Ilium vicit pater, / vos diruistis" ["My father conquered Troy; the lesser task of pillage and destruction is your own."]. And so, various aspects of the Racinian depiction of Pyrrhus — firm, fearless, but without attaining the level of an unquestioned "hero" — parallel the Senecan portrait.

Oreste has no particular Senecan counterpart. There does not exist in the *Troades* or indeed elsewhere in the Senecan repertory, a person whose general characteristics and function in the play resemble those of Racine's Oreste. And yet this character has a personal sentiment, a self-awareness of the kind already encountered in Hecuba, Oedipus, Phaedra, and many other creations of Seneca. Oreste is the principal male example of this in Racine, Phèdre, of course, being the female.

From the very outset Oreste admits that he has surrendered to his passion — which is his destiny: "Je me livre en aveugle au destin qui m'entraîne" (98). At the end, fully cognizant that his arrival caused the catastrophic chain of events, he cries out to the cruel gods (1618-1619), "J'étois né pour servir d'exemple à ta colère, / Pour être du malheur un modèle accompli." And so immediately preceding his fit of madness Oreste becomes fully aware of his function in the universe of the Greeks and the Trojans. He knows from the beginning, however, that his actions are central, and that whatever he does will have repercussions. His self-consciousness grows slowly throughout, until the final cry of pathetic despair (1620), "Hé bien, je meurs content, et *mon sort est rempli*" (italics mine).

This sense of responsibility, this profound introspection on the part of Oreste shows the extent to which Seneca and Racine have a common dramatic ground. Such a type of self-awareness constitutes the basis of Senecan characterization. The reason Racine had recourse to Seneca for such central figures as Andromaque and Phèdre is, therefore, that he saw, amidst the Seneca population, characters endowed with a quality which would lend the desired vitality to his own drama.

The way in which Racine's characters surpass Seneca's may be appreciated by considering this very same trait of introspection. For, while there exists in a Senecan play one person who is responsible, and is aware of it, in a Racinian tragedy all the major characters reveal this awareness of self, not only the person directly accountable for the catastrophe. The explanation derives from the fact that Racine's tragic universe is a rather crowded one in comparison to Seneca's: the French plays concern the actions and interactions of several tormented souls, while the Latin ones treat, in general, the personal disaster of one individual, ruined by unbridled emotion or the whims of fate.

A further derivative of the lucidity found in Racinian characters is the verbal self-control they exhibit. Racine's figures are capable, sooner or later, of understanding their own motives (even though they may often attempt to impose a temporary blindness on themselves), and their struggle becomes all the more frustrating and hopeless for it. Consequently, although their outcries reflect a tragic pain surely as profound as that felt by Seneca's characters, they realize the futility of self-lamentation and they yield to it only at critical moments. Further, their desire to avoid debasing their image in the eyes of the superior being, the beloved, acts as a deterrent to the kind of lengthy, exaggerated, and often degrading declarations with which Seneca's tragedies are replete — one might say that Racine's characters have their own personal interpretation of *bienséances*. Finally, the rigid classical form exacted by French tragedy serves to contain the lyrical moments of intensity so that as a result the perfect counterbalancing of form (conservative) and content (explosive) assures

Racine of avoiding the pitfall of Senecan and French Renaissance tragedy: melodrama in which content clearly dominates form.

From the very beginning or his career, Racine sought to focus the spectator's attention on characters who feel themselves guilty and responsible, as, for example, Jocaste in *La Thébaïde,* who is fully aware of her part in the evil that has befallen her descendants. This was also the characterization that Seneca gave to Jocasta in both the *Phoenissae* and to a lesser extent in *Oedipus*. Though not the best developed nor the most important, Jocaste is the first character in the extant Racinian repertory whose model was in all probability found in Seneca.

Furthermore, when, in *La Thébaïde,* Jocaste proposes that Polynice might turn his ambitions to the conquest of other kingdoms, she expresses herself through Seneca-imitated sentiments (1147-1150). Once the idea is rejected, she recalls the curse upon the House of Laius and its ruling member (1153-1158) which imitates verses 648-649 of the *Phoenissae,* a passage that contains the awful truth, "Sceptra Thebano fuit / impune nulli gerere" ["No Theban hath e'er borne sceptre without penalty"]. It is this conception of hereditary responsibility for evil which has tormented Jocaste and which lies at the very heart of the conflict of *La Thébaïde.*

Polynice's reply (1159-1162) underlines his stubborn nature and his consuming hatred when he states that he prefers death among the kings to life as a subject. This is precisely the basic sentiment expressed in the *Phoenissae* (651-652), "... est tanti mihi / cum regibus iacere." ["'Tis worth the price, methinks, to lie with kings."] Lines 651-652 of the *Phoenissae,* though attributed in corrected modern versions to Eteocles, were usually ascribed to Polynices in the texts of Seneca available in the seventeenth century.

Jocaste, in the act of going off to end her acute feeling of despair, hurls at her sons the bitter charge to kill each other and thus surpass the crimes of their forebears. In this passage (1179-1183) the movement and several of the expressions are quite similar to those verses of the *Phoenissae*'s first fragment wherein Oedipus bitterly urges his progeny on to "greater" exploits (334-338):

agite, o propago cara, generosam indolem
probate factis, gloriam ac laudes meas
superate et aliquid facite propter quod patrem
adhuc iuvet vixisse. facietis, scio:
sic estis orti.

["Go on, dear offspring, prove your noble breeding by your deeds; surpass my fame and praises and do some deed whereat your [father may rejoice that he has lived till now. You will do it, I know: of such mind were you born."]

By the end of Act IV not only Jocaste but also the brothers have left the stage, never to return. In his treatment of Polynice and Étéocle Racine leans toward Rotrou and away from Seneca in that he chooses to give the more volatile personality to Polynice. In what remains of the *Phoenissae* Eteocles stands out as the more vicious and stubborn of the two. In following Rotrou's lead Racine has added an extra touch of *vraisemblance* to his play, for we can easily imagine that the resentment and bitterness of the exile would make him implacable, whereas the affection and arguments of Antigone and Jocaste would perhaps have taken some of the edge off Étéocle's hatred, but not, it would seem, to the point where he consents to let the people decide who should reign.

In its characterization, Racine's following play, *Alexandre le Grand*, is undoubtedly his poorest basically because his figures prove to be as shallow and one-dimensional as those, for example, in Seneca's *Hercules Furens*. Ephestion's function is that of a messenger and confidant-companion to Alexandre, and he begins the line of minor figures with relatively important roles in the plot which will culminate in the indispensible part played by Oenone in *Phèdre*. *La Thébaïde*'s Polynice has a direct descendant in Porus, who may be more reserved and apparently more noble, but who is surely a "flatter" character than Polynice. Antigone's heir is Axiane, but the former's plight is pitiful and hence occasionally moving. But of the six figures in *Alexandre*, Axiane has the best chance of being considered lifelike.

Taxile and Alexandre appear to be the representations of sentiments: Taxile is weakness, Alexandre magnanimity itself. Just as Seneca had done in *Hercules Furens*, Racine permits his hero but little time in view of the audience — a technique which is, however, in keeping with his apparent intention to portray the hero as a noble, generous, even modest being. Since this conception is fundamentally anti-Racinian, Alexandre himself (and the play in general) succeeds in being not only "bad Corneille," [10] but also "bad Racine." Racine's goals seem to be confused: in creating Alexandre he wishes to present, at one and the same time, the supreme conqueror, worthy of our admiration (in typical Senecan and Cornelian fashion), [11] and an individual whose lust for personal glory brings death and devastation to the whole world.

Curiously enough, this last aspect of Alexandre's characterization finds a reflection in *Hercules Furens* in which the supposed benefactor of mankind, Hercules, is responsible for the carnage which fills the play's central divisions. In both plays, therefore, we are confronted with a potentially admirable hero, whose appetites and ambitions are so destructive that the plays may be read as a tragic comment on the vanity of all human effort.

Britannicus, in turn, exhibits techniques of characterization shared by Racine and Seneca, principally in the figure of Néron. We must hasten to add that the Latin play in question *(Octavia)* is not thought to be authentic, and so if there exists an influence, it was exerted by a pseudo-Senecan tragedy.

The historical atmosphere that supports Racine's characterization has an unusual importance in *Britannicus* because he was attempting to refute the charge that he had no historical sense, and to beat Corneille at his own game: tragedy with a Roman setting. Consequently, Racine chose his historical detail carefully from Juvenal (whose contribution is not important), Tacitus (who furnished most of the information), and Seneca. (Just as Corneille had borrowed from Seneca's *De Clementia* for one of his celebrated Roman plays, *Cinna,* so Racine reverts to

---

[10] On page 191, vol. I, of the Pléiade edition of Racine's *Œuvres Complètes*, Raymond Picard refers to Porus' characterization as "du mauvais Corneille." Surely the statement can be applied to the whole play.

[11] In 1665, the date of *Alexandre*'s representation, Corneille had already returned from his "retreat" and was once again the key figure in drama circles. He was, therefore, the one whose formula might hold the key to success for an ambitious young playwright.

the same prose work of Seneca, and, to an even greater extent, to *Octavia*, for the purpose of giving authentic flavor to his own Rome-situated drama.)

Although Racine does refer in his preface to a passage concerning Junie in Chapter VIII of Seneca's *Apocolokyntosis*,[12] he does not elect to mention what *Britannicus* owes to *Octavia*. This was to be expected, for, if Racine had already (in *La Thébaïde* and *Andromaque*) studiously concealed his debt to Seneca, how could he possibly bring himself to admit his indebtedness to a pseudo-Senecan work?[13]

The historical background of *Britannicus* succeeds in concentrating the spectator's attention on the deeds and personality of the central figure, the legendary madman, Néron. Racine's sketching of Néron, at the play's outset, as hesitant and insecure, resembles the portrayal of Nero in *Octavia*. Moreover, in the latter play, the passion of Nero for Poppaea is the source of the bloodshed. Racine makes his own Néron *amoureux* and the emperor's frustrated desire is the immediate cause of his crimes, which begin with the poisoning of his rival Britannicus — the first step down the road to a reign of terror that will irrevocably mark Néron as the mad despot of history. The difference between *Octavia* and *Britannicus* lies in Racine's portraying Néron's *birth* to infamy, while the author of the Latin play depicts the *consequences* of that initiation to evil. Yet, though the points of departure are different, the characters of Nero and Agrippina appear in both tragedies as principal figures in a conflict of wills.

---

[12] See the Mesnard edition, II, 252, where Racine states, "Cette Junie étoit jeune, belle, et comme dit Sénèque, *festivissima omnium puellarum*."

[13] This argumentation is obviously based on the assumption that Racine himself considered Octavia spurious. I can find no concrete evidence which supports — or refutes — this theory. However, Léon Herrmann has come to the same conclusion as I, and he also observes ("*Octavie*, source de *Britannicus*," *Bulletin de l'Association Guillaume Budé* [April, 1925], 28): "Il suffira d'avoir indiqué que, dans *Britannicus*, Racine s'est plus écarté des historiens latins et plus inspiré d'*Octavie* qu'on ne le croit communément." To the point, Pierre Robert (*La Poétique de Racine*, Paris, 1891, p. 87) notes, "Mais le drame de Racine doit être surtout une lutte de passions, et non pas une peinture historique." This is certainly the case, and it would be natural to expect that Racine would therefore look to a work which concerned the interplay of emotions (as in a drama) to supplement a purely historical source like Tacitus.

Seneca and Octavia also have counterparts in *Britannicus*. Though Sénèque as a character never appears, his presence is felt *in absentia* through his influence on the young emperor. Moreover, Racine's Burrhus, who plays the role equivalent to Seneca in *Octavia*, is made to speak with the same conviction and to express many of the same sentiments.[14] Octavia herself has no equivalent in name in *Britannicus*. However, in his article on *Octavia*, Herrmann points out that Octavie is mentioned in several instances in Racine's tragedy as if, though absent from the stage, she were just "dans la coulisse."[15] Her proximity contributes to the psychological local color of the play. Furthermore, there is a sharp resemblance of the chaste, tender, and somehow melancholy Octavia to Junie, who has the same traits and who also first detects the criminal side of Néron.[16] Quite possibly, then, Junie is not merely the *jeune première* to be found in many seventeenth-century dramas. Perhaps she owes her character traits to a historical figure of some importance.

Bajazet[17] too contains a character who appears to have been formed in a Senecan mold: Roxane. She shares several essential qualities with the sensual Phaedra of Seneca (and it should be recalled that Seneca's literary preoccupation with physical desire borders on the obsessive), and she is no less relentless in her pursuit of the loved one. Indeed she will even plead with Bajazet,

---

[14] See verses 786-790, 1330, 1335-1336, and 1355-1365 of *Britannicus* in which Burrhus echoes the character Seneca of *Octavia*, and in which Néron sharply replies. Burrhus offers advice that is really too sage, coming from a man of action, an old soldier. While his fidelity, indeed his blind loyalty to the emperor would be characteristic of a former legionnaire, Burrhus' sententious mouthings make one think of the court philosopher Seneca. As Racine has drawn him, Burrhus appears to be a mixture of the strongest ingredients of both imperial tutors, Burrhus and Seneca.

[15] "Octavie, source de *Britannicus*," p. 16. Herrmann explains that, in spite of verse 83 of *Britannicus* ("A peine parle-t-on de la triste Octavie"), people do indeed speak of her: 465-484; 530, 532, 534, 595-598, etc.; 784; 815-830, 880, etc.; 1215, 1450, etc. Néron also has Britannicus held in Octavie's apartment (1081); Junie and Agrippine go there before the death of Britannicus (1568-1570); finally, Junie pretends to seek her out after the crime ("Elle feint de passer chez la triste Octavie," 1724).

[16] See *Britannicus*, 415, 417-423, 610 ff., and *Octavia*, 49, 70-71, 79.

[17] Between *Britannicus* and *Bajazet*, two plays which possess Senecan characteristics were produced (both in 1670): Quinault's *Bellérophon* and the anonymous *Deuterie Reine de France*.

as when she cries (538, 541), "Bajazet, écoutez; je sens que je vous aime / ... Ne désespérez point une amante en furie." This recalls the supplication of Phaedra, who throws herself at Hippolytus' feet while declaring (668-671):

> respersa nulla labe et intacta, innocens
> tibi mutor uni. certa descendi ad preces:
> finem hic dolori faciet aut vitae dies.
> miserere amantis.

> ["... Without a spot
> Of Sin, unstained and innocent, was I;
> And thou alone hast wrought the change in me.
> See, at thy feet I kneel and pray, resolved
> This day shall end my misery or life.
> Oh, pity her who loves thee...."]

None of Racine's predecessors or contemporaries infuse into their Phaedra character this excitement generated by a strong physical desire leading to a profound despair.[18] Fauste, in *L'Innocent Malheureux* (1639) of François de Grenaille does declare herself in a fashion analogous to Seneca's Phaedra,[19] but the total effect remains unconvincing and hollow. The Phèdre of Gilbert (*Hypolite ou le Garçon Insensible*, 1647) is just the fiancée of Thésée, and she seems more basically concerned with preserving her self-integrity than with attracting Hypolite. The sixth episode of *Les Nouvelles Françaises ou les Divertissements de la Princesse Aurélie* (1657) by Segrais contains a situation analogous to

---

[18] Those contemporary historical sources responsible for local color and décor in *Bajazet* have been examined by W. G. Moore ("Le Bajazet de Racine," *RSH*, avril-juin 1949, 69-82), who opts for an oral authority (M. de Césy), and by Georges May ("La Genèse de Bajazet," *MLQ*, June, 1948, 152-164), who rather relies on a written document (the French translation of Paul Rycaut's *The History of the Present State of the Ottoman Empire*, London, 1669).

[19] The reason for this is that Grenaille evidently imitated Seneca. In the Préface to *L'Innocent Malheureux* Grenaille notes: "L'*Hippolyte* de Sénèque est pareillement un chef d'œuvre sur lequel on peut tirer l'idée de toute sorte de beaux ouvrages tragiques, & la conformité de son sujet avec le mien peut avoir produit en plusieurs endroits de la ressemblance en la forme. Quoy qu'il en soit, je ne l'ay pas voulu lire de nouveau en composant cette pièce, & s'il y a quelques traits pareills [sic], je suis bien aise d'être disciple d'un si grand Maistre et de suivre au moins de loin celuy que je voudrois approcher."

Bajazet's including the very names employed by Racine, but the resemblance ends there, for Segrais' lifeless creations could have contributed little to Racine's characterizations, even if one assumes that Racine knew the *nouvelle* (doubted by Dr. Moore, affirmed by Professor May). Finally, Sténobée, the female lead in Quinault's *Bellérophon* (1670) possesses little of the real torment found in Phaedra and Roxane, nor does she ever declare her passion to Bellérophon.

Racine's debt to predecessors in *Bajazet* consists primarily in his delineation of Bajazet, who resembles the Hyppolytus character of earlier plays by the general nature of his situation (forbidden love, political subordination to the queen who desires him). Racine also incorporates into the basic Phaedra legend the real object of the young man's affection. [20] This same triadic construction will also appear in Racine's *Phèdre*. In fact, both *Bajazet* (II, 1) and *Phèdre* (II, 5) contain another structural similarity; declaration scenes which resemble not only each other, but also the equivalent moment in Seneca's *Phaedra* (646-718). [21] Moreover, one can see similarities in the nature of each play's heroine, and in her problem. These parallelisms between the two Racinian plays on the one hand, and the Senecan tragedy on the other make one suspect (1) that both Roxane and Phèdre are indebted to Seneca's Phaedra, and (2) that *Bajazet* and the figure Roxane in particular may have served as preliminary sketches for Racine's *Phèdre*.

---

[20] The first French version of the Phaedra theme containing such a role is the thirteenth-century poem *La Châtelaine de Vergi*. But the more proximate source for this character, within the Phèdre tradition, is found in Constance of Tristan's *La Mort de Crispe* (1645).

[21] Although the circumstances differ, several verses spoken by Bajazet on the one hand, and Phèdre on the other, present a striking similarity. Compare:

> De quoi nous a servi cette indigne contrainte?
> Je meurs plus tard: voilà tout le fruit de ma feinte.
> Je vous l'avois prédit; mais vous l'avez voulu.
> *(Bajazet, 669-671)*

> Je te l'ai prédit; mais tu n'as pas voulu.
> Sur mes justes remords tes pleurs ont prévalu.
> Je mourois ce matin digne d'être pleurée;
> J'ai suivi tes conseils, je meurs deshonorée.
> *(Phèdre, 835-838)*

The most striking aspect of a comparison of Bajazet with Phaedra is the similar self-awareness of the heroines. Both are aware of the desperate nature of their love, but must give expression to it regardless of the consequences. Both women are eventually frustrated, and they consciously contribute to the destruction of the loved one and eventually of themselves. John Lapp has perceived the introspective nature of the main figure of *Bajazet* and compares her with Phèdre, in that "both heroines are agonizingly conscious of the impossibility of their position." [22] And so, for some time before the actual composition of Phèdre, Racine may have been thinking of creating a female character with many of Phaedra's traits, and Roxane would thus be a kind of first draft. [23]

Once the distinct possibility of Seneca's role in *Bajazet* is entertained, the object of a long-standing literary inquest may be more accurately redefined. Eugène Vinaver has outlined the problem in this fashion: "Le poète qui déclarait inutile 'les morts et le sang' et cherchait à abolir l'intrigue au profit du pathétique, donne, deux ans après, une pièce à complot qui s'achève sur un affreux massacre. 'On n'entre point dans les raisons de cette grande tuerie,' disait la judicieuse et, comme nous dirions aujourd'hui, l'impressionniste Madame de Sévigné. Après trois siècles d'exégèse, ces raisons nous échappent." [24] I suggest that the question should be rephrased thus: Why did Racine write *Bérénice*? Racine's dramatic efforts immediately before *Bérénice* possess the violence of a Senecan play, and the tumultuous happenings of *Bajazet* fall into the same pattern. Surely, then, we should consider the Sophoclean simplicity of *Bérénice* as the exception.

Racine's composition of *Bérénice* probably constitutes another step in the progression of the Racine-Corneille rivalry. After pointing out the emphasis on simplicity and *vraisemblance* in

---

[22] *Aspects of Racinian Tragedy*, p. 23.
[23] E. B. O. Borgerhoff, in his *Freedom of French Classicism* (Princeton, 1950, p. 168), seems to share this point of view though stating it in more general terms: "One comes always finally to *Phèdre*. I believe that from *La Thébaïde* forward, Racine was preparing to write it, and though he did not want to say so outright it is everywhere evident in the preface that he considered it his best play."
[24] *Racine et la Poésie Tragique* (Paris, 1951), p. 69.

Racine's preface to *Bérénice*, Raymond Picard concludes: "On serait presque tenté de se demander si le poète n'a pas été amené à définir ainsi sa position, autant à cause de sa rivalité avec Corneille que pour des raisons d'esthétique dramatique." [25] And so, whether by reason of personal conflict or because of a desire to emulate the uncomplicated patterns of a Sophocles, Racine created *Bérénice*. Once this experiment had been placed before the public, Racine seemed to feel little obligation to adhere to his newly defined principles, and, it seems to me, he reverted to a Senecan model for much of *Bajazet*, with a particular view to profiting from the surge of interest in *turquerie*.

In *Bérénice* the characters are analogous to Seneca's in their power of introspection, but Racine has stepped forward into an area not familiar to Seneca: historical self-consciousness. Titus and Bérénice are aware from the outset of the particular relationship which exists between them. But as the drama progresses, both of them, but more acutely Titus, become conscious of the role they play in history, and this adds a further, more formidable obstacle to the satisfaction of their love. All of scene 6 of Act V concerns this particular kind of self-awareness — of one's reputation, obligations, and one's historical being (1394-1396, 1409-1414):

> Ma gloire inexorable à toute heure me suit:
> Sans cesse elle présente à mon âme étonnée
> L'empire incompatible avec votre hyménée...
>
> Je me suis vu, Madame, enseigner ce chemin
> Et par plus d'un héros et par plus d'un Romain:
> Lorsque trop de malheurs ont lassé leur constance,
> Ils ont tous expliqué cette persévérance
> Dont le sort s'attachoit à les persécuter,
> Comme un ordre secret de n'y plus résister.

Finally, this conception renders the famous last lines of Bérénice all the more apt (1502-1504):

---

[25] *La Carrière de Jean Racine* (Paris, 1956), p. 165.

> Adieu: servons tous trois d'exemple à l'univers
> De l'amour la plus tendre et la plus malheureuse
> Dont il puisse garder l'histoire douloureuse.

In the case of *Bérénice*, therefore, individual self-knowledge, and a pessimism concerning the futility of human attempts at union in love mark Racine's affinity with Seneca.

In *Iphigénie* Racine borrowed considerably, though it is imitation of the Greeks which, by and large, served him. There does exist, among all the passages of imitation, one which is probably of Senecan origin. A comparison of verses 229-232 of the *Troades* with *Iphigénie*, 163-168, will make clear the suggestive value of the Senecan passage to Racine:

> haec tánta clades gentium ac tantus pavor,
> sparsae tot urbes turbinis vasti modo
> alterius esset gloria ac summum decus;
> iter est Achillis.

["This great overthrow of nations, this widespread terror, all these cities wrecked as by a tornado's blast, to another could have been glory and the height of fame; to Achilles they were but deeds upon the way."]

> D'un courage naissant sont-ce là les essais?
> Quels triomphes suivront de si nobles succès!
> La Thessalie entière, ou vaincue ou calmée,
> Lesbos meme conquise en attendant l'armée,
> De toute autre valeur éternels monuments,
> Ne sont d'Achille oisif que les amusements.

Another point of interest lies in the portrayal of Agamemnon. While the broad lines of his characterization are from the Euripidean *Iphigenia at Aulis*, there is a moment in Act IV (scene 8) where Agamemnon reveals a Senecan trait: he wavers between two courses of action; indeed, the reason for the entire scene is to emphasize this indecision. The pose of the person caught in a moment of indecision before a vital resolution is a Senecan device, and Racine makes splendid use of it here. Euripides, it should be noted, does not put his character through such hesitation and soul-searching before reaching a decision.

Ulysses too may derive his fundamental traits of craftiness and cruelty from Seneca. W. B. Stanford notes, in "On some references to Ulysses in French literature from Du Bellay to Fénelon," [26] that Racine's opinion of Ulysses in his *Remarques sur l'Odyssée d'Homère* (1662) is highly sympathetic. The change in his view between 1662 and 1674 may have been caused by Racine's increased sensitivity to Ulysses' unpopular image in the *Troades*, which contains a scene concerning the deceitful Ulysses already imitated by Racine in *Bajazet* and *Mithridate*. [27]

The last point worthy of mention is that Racine, I suspect, was trying to render a copy of Seneca's Medea in his portrayal of Eriphile, and the imitation succeeds despite the relative brevity of Eriphile's role. In this character there exists that same burning love, that same jealousy, that particular thirst (really, a need) for vengeance, which characterize Seneca's Medea.

Just like Medea, Eriphile takes pleasure in bringing ill, and she is therefore similarly frightening when she schemes. Verses like the following are strictly Medean (1143-1144), "Rentrons. Et pour troubler un hymen odieux, / Consultons des fureurs qu'autorisent les Dieux." There seems to be an infernal air to such utterances, recalling Medea's incantations.

Eriphile's craving for revenge is well communicated as she closes the second act with these words (756-766):

> Dieux, qui voyez ma honte, où dois-je me cacher?
> Orgueilleuse rivale, on t'aime, et tu murmures?
> Souffrirai-je à la fois ta gloire et tes injures? ...
> Et si le sort contre elle à ma haine se joint,
> Je saurai profiter de cette intelligence
> Pour ne pas pleurer seule et mourir sans vengeance.

To the last of the preceding lines I will add another which typifies the independence of Eriphile and her consciousness of her situation (1126), "Je suis et je serai la seule infortunée." The ability to draw upon oneself for great strength and perseverance is, as I have endeavored to show in Part I, a trait wholly Medean.

---

[26] *Studies in Philology*, L (July, 1953), 449-450.

[27] See the next chapter for a discussion of these similar scenes in *Bajazet* and *Mithridate*.

Moreover, the perception of her true condition distinguishes Seneca's creation from the Greek character. Of course, in the case of Eriphile, it is an awareness that she must search for her true self and her rightful place.

Even to the last, Eriphile displays a supreme pride as well as a great deal of courage. Her final words are these (1772-1774):

> Arrête... et ne m'approche pas.
> Le sang de ces héros dont tu me fais descendre
> Sans tes profanes mains saura bien se répandre.

In view of Racine's excellence in female characterization, one could normally expect that he would have tried his skill at presenting the grandest of all female dramatic figures, Medea. Further, I believe that the success of Eriphile, a secondary character, may have encouraged Racine to create a Medea type of greater, and therefore more suitable, magnitude: Athalie.

In *Athalie* the main figure, like Medea, challenges the whole existing order — social for Medea, theological for Athalie. (There are some overtones of theological import in *Medea*, for Jason ends the drama by protesting that there are no gods.) Athalie, the mightiest of all Racinian creations, lashes out at the divinity, no longer content to attack mere humanity. Thus her last curse rings out like a prophecy, to give the impression that, like Nessus, she will exact a posthumous vengeance (1784-1790):

> Que dis-je souhaiter? je me flatte, j'espère
> Qu'indocile à ton joug, fatigué de ta loi,
> Fidèle au sang d'Achab, qu'il a reçu de moi,
> Conforme à son aïeul, à son père semblable,
> On verra de David l'héritier détestable
> Abolir tes honneurs, profaner ton autel,
> Et venger Athalie, Achab et Jézabel. [28]

---

[28] John Lapp ("Racine est-il Sénéquien," p. 132) has suggested the same comparison: "La Médée de l'auteur romain diffère beaucoup du modèle grec. Celle qui selon Créon joint 'une fourberie toute féminine à une force toute virile et à une totale inconscience de l'infâmie' (265-269) nous rappelle à bien des égards Athalie. Mais c'est surtout par l'élément irrationnel de son caractère qu'elle ressemble aux héroïnes raciniennes. On pourrait signaler surtout la tirade où elle oscille entre ses désirs de vengeance et ses sentiments de mère (894-978)."

These are the sentiments of a character, created by Racine, who is Senecan in nature; a strong, almost superhuman villainess, wild in her willingness to crush everything, including herself, in her desire for vengeance. (Let us recall Seneca's preference for revenge themes.) I find it particularly fitting for my investigation, therefore, that the last great character of the Racinian corpus bear the mark of Seneca.

CHAPTER III

STRUCTURE: *BAJAZET* AND *MITHRIDATE*

Bajazet and *Mithridate* are valuable for my purposes because they contain a crucial scene which may be imitative of Seneca, and because *Mithridate* in particular sheds light on a possible affinity between Racine and Seneca in the conception of dramatic structure.

Mithridate may be called a "tragédie de situation" because it is surely not a "tragédie de caractère" where the destructive element arises from within the person himself. In *Mithridate* the characters are masters of their fate, to an even greater extent than was true in a previous Racinian offering, *Alexandre le Grand*. The idea of preserving one's own esteem, and indeed succeeding in that effort, is basic to *Mithridate*.

Mithridate is the story of a hero whose actions shake the worlds of all around him, and even of those who have heard only his name. Like the plays of the Hercules cycle, *Mithridate* is constructed on a monocentric plan. I suggest that, if Racine is indebted to someone for the structure of *Mithridate*, it is chiefly to Seneca, and not to Molière's *L'Avare*, as claimed by Voltaire in the *Préface* to *Marianne*.[1] For example, Mithridate's entrance

---

[1] While it is undeniably true, as Voltaire states in this *Préface* (*Œuvres Complètes*, ed. L. Moland, Paris, 1877, v. II), that the plot of *Mithridate* "est aussi propre à la comédie qu'à la tragédie," I cannot agree that the idea for the trap laid by Mithridate was drawn from *L'Avare*. For, although Racine may have been reminded of the effectiveness of just such a ruse by the appropriate moment of the Molière play (IV, 3), the entire preparation of the Racinian version of the "trap scene" recalls Seneca.

is delayed, as is that of Hercules in *Hercules Furens,* so that when he finally does arrive the effect is greater. Mithridate's return is all the more striking because it is a surprise: it will be remembered that the device of spreading false news (already employed in *Bajazet,* and to be used again in *Phèdre*) has been inserted in the first act, and Mithridate is assumed to be dead. The action has been proceeding from this assumption, and the corrected news of the fleet's arrival jolts Monime, Pharnace, and Xipharès back into their roles as subordinates whose fate depends greatly upon the king.

An analogous situation occurs in *Hercules Furens* where Hercules is presumed dead or lost, and his family is consequently mistreated by the tyrant who seeks to usurp the hero's throne. When Hercules returns, the dramatic universe relocates its center, and everything revolves around the mightiest of mortals.

Mithridate, as Racine presents him, has also attained heroic stature, and he proves himself worthy of his reputation. From his opening lines he presents the image of a hard, suspicious, and extremely clever individual, whose intimations instill fear. For example, once the spectator is acquainted with the personality of Mithridate, the following lines, which seem to be little more than an indulgent rebuke, take on a stronger, menacing tone, made emphatic by the sarcasm of the last verse (423-427):

> Princes, quelque raisons que vous me puissiez dire,
> Votre devoir ici n'a point dû vous conduire,
> Ni vous faire quitter, en de si grands besoins,
> Vous le Pont, vous Colchos, confiés à vos soins.
> Mais vous avez pour juge un père qui vous aime.

Thus, while Seneca's Hercules seems to derive his superiority from his physical force, Racine's creation excels in both physical and mental capacities, that is, Racine's hero combines the legendary valor of a Hercules with the equally famous cunning of a Ulysses.

When, indeed, Mithridate desires to learn the truth, he has recourse, not to force, but to his wits. He schemes to ensnare Monime by lying to her and watching her reactions; and this particular moment (III, 6) immediately recalls the Ulysses —

Andromacha scene in the *Troades*[2] where Andromacha unsuccessfully attempts to conceal Astyanax from the Greeks.

Similarly in *Bajazet* the event which determines the catastrophe is the trap set by Roxane for Atalide. The circumstances are these: Roxane, at first unaware of Bajazet's affection for Atalide, grows suspicious, and in her soliloquy (III, 7) expresses her fears and doubts, remaining suspended between belief and skepticism until, in the next scene, Zatime informs her of the arrival of the Sultan's personal messenger. Roxane then returns to practical considerations, and makes her decision (1119-1122):

> Ils ont beau se cacher. L'amour le plus discret
> Laisse par quelque marque échapper son secret.
> Observons Bajazet; étonnons Atalide;
> Et couronnons l'amant, ou perdons le perfide.

The scene of the *Troades* (525-735) just noted in connection with *Mithridate* may again have been of service to Racine, this time in *Bajazet*. In one of the tensest moments in all of Senecan drama, Ulysses demands that Andromacha deliver Astyanax to him, but, in an impassioned discourse, she claims that her son has already died. Andromacha is so persuasive that even the wily Ulysses is temporarily convinced. However, he reverts to form, and attempts to uncover the truth by deceiving Andromacha and then carefully watching her reaction. He even expresses the heart of his scheme in much the same commonplace phraseology just encountered in *Bajazet*, for he says (614-615), "Veritas numquam perit. / scrutare matrem..." ["Truth is never lost. Watch the mother."].

Racine may have remembered certain aspects of the Ulysses-Andromacha encounter while composing *Mithridate* because he was about to construct a scene of similar content, and could profit from Seneca's example (as well as his own in *Bajazet*). The parallel scenes in *Mithridate* and the *Troades* are even prepared in the same manner. Both of the warriors (Mithridate-Ulysses) are

---

[2] The third episode, particularly verses 614-705. Though the "trap scene" does exist in Seneca, it does not in French version of the Mithridate story chronologically closest to Racine's play: *La Mort de Mithridate* (1635) by La Calprenède.

renowned for their cunning and skepticism, and the spectator witnesses an extraordinary event: the apparent acceptance, by these perceptive individuals, of false declarations. However, in a short aside, each one awakens to the possibility of deception, returns to his suspicions, and resolves to discover the truth by a ruse. In the *Troades* Ulysses expresses himself in these words (607-618):

> quid agis, Vlixe? Danaidae credent tibi...
> nunc advoca astus, anime, nunc fraudes, dolos,
> nunc totum Vlixen; veritas numquam perit.
>   ... ingenio est opus.

> ["What doest thou, Ulysses? The Danai will believe thy word, but whose word, thou? ... Now, my heart, summon up thy craft, thy tricks, thy wiles, now all Ulysses, truth is always to be discovered.... Now I have need of skill."]

Mithridate's words, which are similar to those just cited, are these (1022-1034):

>   Mais par où commencer?
> Qui m'en éclaircira? quels témoins? quel indice? ...
> Le ciel en ce moment m'inspire un artifice...
> Feignons; et de son cœur, d'un vain espoir flatté,
> Par un mensonge adroit tirons la vérité.

Racine utilizes the device of the strategem in exactly the same place in *Mithridate* as it had been used in the *Troades:* the latter part of the third act.[3] But in Racine this is not mere suspense, for Mithridate's basic character is skilfully revealed through it: he shows himself to be shrewd, distrustful, and jealous. Yet even

---

[3] It is the Mithridate of the beginning of Act III who recalls Seneca for Ettore Paratore ("Les Préjugés les plus pernicieux...," 339-340): "Si nous nous penchons sur *Mithridate*, nous voyons que la première scène du troisième acte, cette véritable conférence que le vieux roi fait à ses fils pour leur confier son projet de se ruer sur Rome révèle le même goût de l'érudition géographique et historique, le même penchant aux exhibitions savantes qui caractérisent le théâtre de Sénèque: que l'on songe au long discours que Jocaste adresse à Polynice dans les *Phoenissae* afin de l'inciter à se pourvoir d'un autre royaume dans les régions de l'Asie."

after discovering Monime's true sentiments he continues to possess fatherly affection and a certain faith, in spite of himself, in his favorite son. Mithridate cannot bring himself to lose all confidence in Xipharès, and to condemn him — which would be the expected reaction from the man hardened by long, bitter, and ruthless combat. The sympathetic side of Mithridate comes to light, therefore, through this scene. This kind of difference exists almost everywhere that one discovers a Racine-Seneca relationship: that is, whereas Seneca's use of a theme or technique is limited to a single goal, Racine's dramatic sense permits him to give multiple purpose to what might be considered theatrical necessity.

Finally, one should note that there remains another side to the Racine-Seneca "partnership" which demonstrates that the Senecan influence is not always of happy consequence. If, as has been suggested, Racine is following Seneca's model in structuring *Mithridate* tightly around the central figure, one could then ascribe one of the play's weaknesses to the imitation of Seneca: and that consists in the use of indistinguishable minor characters. Arbate, for instance, has a definite function in the drama. But such is the strong focus on the hero and his conflicts that Arbate is completely deprived of any personality that might generate an interest capable of detracting attention from the central plot. This kind of construction remains a cardinal defect in Senecan drama, and I believe that Racine may have fallen heir to it in this play in an attempt to structure his work after a Senecan fashion: monocentrically. Nowhere in *Mithridate* does one encounter a character of secondary importance so well-defined as Narcisse or Oenone. Rather *Mithridate* introduces people who, as in Seneca, fulfill their purpose and disappear.

Senecan structure appears to have been utilized in several instances by Racine. The whole structure of *La Thébaïde* reveals a thorough knowledge of the strengths and evident flaws of Senecan drama, especially of the *Phoenisase*. Instead of exhausting the material of the fragmented Senecan play in the first two acts, as Rotrou had done in his *Antigone*, Racine selects and places carefully throughout *La Thébaïde* those details which he feels would increase his play's power. By this type of integration,

Racine avoids Rotrou's pitfall, that of having two centers of interest, one taken from Seneca's drama and the other of Rotrou's own creation, with some Sophoclean traces.

Racine employs Antigone, who appears in all five acts, as the unifying force in his tragedy. She ties together the various threads of the plot, because of her intimate connection with them: the Polynice-Étéocle quarrel, the ambitions of Créon, and, of course, the love of Hémon for herself. The author makes Antigone somewhat more realistic, while binding her closely to the problem of fratricide, by infusing in her a definite preference for the exile Polynice, not only because of the justice of his claim but also because it would be expected of a woman to take sides with the "outcast."

Moreover, when Antigone leaves the stage for the final time (V, 3), the play is in its last moments. The deaths of the brothers, Jocaste, and Hémon have been made known by that time, and with the expected demise of Antigone, there remains but one thread to be sewn into the whole of the plot: Créon's fate. It is doubtless a coincidence, but curious nevertheless, that Racine views Antigone's function as quite similar to Seneca's Antigona: she unifies the several subplots in Racine, just as Seneca's Antigona is, from what one may judge, the character who would have tied the Oedipus situation (first fragment of the *Phoenissae*) to the quarrel of the brothers (second fragment).

Although the abbreviated condition of the *Phoenissae* precludes any imitation of its total structure by Racine in *La Thébaïde,* it remains clear that Racine borrowed freely from Seneca, despite the appearance to the contrary that he wanted to convey in his preface to *La Thébaïde*.

Alexandre le Grand apparently owes little to Seneca if we limit our examination to the obvious features of story, theme, and verse borrowings. Yet, even if the usual kinds of influence are much less pronounced, the play, taken as a whole, smacks of Senecan inspiration, and this should not surprise us since the Racinian tragedies that "surround" *Alexandre (La Thébaïde, Andromaque)* bear traces of heavy debt to Seneca.

Of course, the similarity to Corneille must not be overlooked, but there again, Seneca enters the picture, for the subject of

Racine's tragedy is *la clémence d'Alexandre,* just as Corneille had written *Cinna ou la Clémence d'Auguste,* which in the 1648 and 1656 editions had a dedication ("A Monsieur de Montoron") accompanied by the text of Seneca's treatise (*De Clementia,* I, 9) dealing with the magnanimity of Augustus. Thus it may be that Racine had chosen his subject in imitation of Corneille, who, in turn, had borrowed it from Seneca. But again there may exist a more direct connection between Racine and Seneca in *Alexandre.*

In his *Seconde Préface* Racine notes: "... qu'il n'y a pas un vers dans la tragédie qui ne soit à la louange d'Alexandre; que les invectives même de Porus et d'Axiane sont autant d'éloges de la valeur de ce conquérant." [4] Perhaps Racine was conscious of *La Thébaïde*'s major flaw — its lack of tight organization — and hoped to correct this structural error by making one character the very obvious protagonist in *Alexandre.* Therefore the play will be a highly centralized one, its main concern being the generosity of the hero, Alexandre. He is described, glorified, maligned, but remains the focal point until, after two acts and four scenes of dramatic preparation, he enters with these words, which constitute an all too evident attempt at immediate self-characterization (835-836), "Allez, Ephestion. Que l'on cherche Porus; / Qu'on épargne sa vie, et le sang des vaincus." Just as Néron's first act (the exiling of Pallas) will characterize his hardness, so Alexandre's will demonstrate his brand of generosity (a generosity, we should recall, which he puts to effective and selfish use to gain his final victory — a moral triumph over Porus).

If we take up Seneca's *Hercules Furens,* we notice that the same entrance-exit pattern applies to Hercules as to Alexandre: first appearance in the third act, reappearance in the fourth act, domination of the fifth act by his continued presence. Both heroes are presented as demi-gods, indeed Porus even makes an implicit comparison of Hercules and Alexandre by sarcastically lending the latter the former's parentage (572-574):

---

[4] In this same preface Racine quotes from Seneca's *Consolatio ad Helvetiam,* chapter XIII. See the Mesnard edition, I, 532.

> Nous savons que les dieux ne sont pas des tyrans;
> Et de quelque façon qu'un esclave le nomme,
> Le fils de Jupiter passe ici pour un homme.

Further, Alexandre's prowess is described in Act II, scene 1 by Ephestion and Cléofile, just as Megara will evoke the accomplishments of Hercules at the beginning of Act II of *Hercules Furens*. Finally, Hercules enters the play after having returned from hell, and, if Cléofile's prediction holds true, Alexandre's search for conquest will take him inevitably to just such a place (1325-1332):

> Mais quoi, seigneur, toujours guerre sur guerre?
> Cherchez-vous des sujets au delà de la terre?
> Voulez-vous pour témoins de vos faits éclatants
> Des pays inconnus mêmes à leurs habitants?
> Qu'espérez-vous combattre en des climats si rudes?
> Ils vous opposeront de vastes solitudes,
> Des déserts que le ciel refuse d'éclairer,
> Où la nature semble elle-même expirer.

Evidently, then, *Hercules Furens* and *Alexandre le Grand* have points of similarity in the way in which they prepare the hero's entrance, his time upon the stage, even his characterization to a certain extent. The most obvious parallel can be drawn between the central role that the title character plays in each of these tragedies: he is the pivot which permits the whole structure of the drama to turn. In a word, these two tragedies are monocentric, and a common conception of dramatic form may be operative in them.

Racine would return to this same pattern in *Mithridate* in which once again he sought to present a celebrated warrior of antiquity. Racine's powers were surely more developed in 1673, and *Mithridate* is a more interesting play (Louis XIV's favorite, it has been said). But, a similar attention to the central figure — the hero — and an accompanying lack of vigorous characterization in some of the other roles is evident, as in *Alexandre*.[5]

---

[5] Marcel Gutwirth comes to approximately the same conclusion in "La Problématique de l'Innocence dans le théâtre de Racine" (*RSH*, 106, avril-juin 1962), p. 193, "... *Alexandre* dont *Mithridate* offre une réédition en plus sombre...."

Paradoxically, the two monocentric plays of Racine are among his least passionate tragedies. In Seneca the close concentration on the principal figure is the occasion for much introspection which results in the excessive expression of sentiment. The Senecan monologues serve, therefore, a melodramatic purpose. *Alexandre le Grand* and *Mithridate,* on the other hand, have relatively little self-examination, the reason being that Racine apparently does not wish to concentrate on Alexandre's or Mithridate's inner workings as much as on their feats of heroism. Neither of these two heroes has reason to complain at length in the manner of a Hercules, and so in Racine the portrayal of passion's ravages is not the point of his two plays' tightly concentrated structure. Rather he prefers to focus his artistic spotlight on the superior military and moral qualities of his central figures. Characteristically, Racine's own needs determine his interpretation and utilization of a Senecan device.

Fundamentally, the reason why Senecan or Seneca-inspired tragedy can furnish elements of importance and variety to Racine lies in the general similarity in the conception of dramatic structure. Seneca prefers to begin his drama at a delayed starting point, close to the moment of crisis; his choice for the climactic moment — invariably late in the play (the fourth or fifth acts) — indicates his desire to create a mood of surging emotional tension which he attempts to heighten to the point where explosion results, and where the emotional — and physical — fracturing is all the greater. Seneca does not often succeed in attaining the desired ever-increasing effect because of his monotonous tone, but his ideas on the structure of a tragedy are clear, and, as I have described them in general terms, they might also compose a definition of Racine's conception.

There are particular points of identity in the two conceptions. The prologue in Seneca serves as an exposition that is usually complete and clear, as does the first act in Racine. But the latter begins even closer to the point of maximum intensity (a prologue would be not only time-wasting but *invraisemblable*). Racine's first act contains much more than mere exposition of details and atmosphere, since it introduces the spectator to the movement of a plot which, it would appear, had been going on for some time before the curtain's rise. Thus the "Oui" or "Quoi?" which constitutes the opening expression of certain Racinian dramas creates the impression that the spectator has penetrated the fourth wall of the room depicted on stage, and he is therefore in a position to grasp the actions and to appreciate the motives of the characters from the outset.

In Part I, I mentioned the "return" scene as especially central to the climax of a Senecan tragedy. Racine has some scenes of the same nature: the return of Thesée, the arrival of Orcan in *Bajazet* (which is tantamount to the return of the Sultan), and the appearance of Mithridate. The first two figures make their entrance at the point chosen by Seneca for his returning characters: the third act — to precipitate the crisis of the fourth act. Since Mithridate plays the central role, Racine chooses to allow him ample time on stage to express and reveal himself, and so the news of his arrival reaches the two brothers and Monime in the fifth scene of Act I.

A final structural analogy worth mentioning at this point is the *liaison des scènes*. In Seneca this device results more accidentally than consciously: given the monocentricity of his dramas, it is likely that many of his scenes will be linked to their successor by the continued presence of the main character. Furthermore, this emphasis on one figure produces a dramatic society which is paradoxically not tight-knit, that is, usually only one or two of the individuals are deeply affected by the action, because there exists a minimum of interaction. Though there may well be a protagonist and an antagonist of sorts in every Senecan play, the spectator's attention is so constantly directed to the condition of the central character that the action seems really to concern him exclusively.

On the other hand, the *liaison des scènes* in Racine remains a convenient structural technique, inherited from the dramatic tradition, which serves him admirably by underscoring the paradox of his creations: like the compartments of their dramatic cadre, the play, Racinian characters are inextricably linked, and their actions have grave consequences for one another; and yet most of them are totally alone, self-centered, incapable of really acknowledging the existence of others. For those who do share, who do love reciprocally (Britannicus-Junie, Antigone-Hémon, Bajazet-Atalide, Bérénice-Titus), fate has decreed that the uniting of the two lovers be impossible, either because of death or its equivalent: ultimate separation.

Because of the suppression of communication in its most fundamental and human sense — that is, love — a world of extreme cruelty is born, where, in one's effort to make contact, if not to dominate, the characters rip and slash at one another with emotional weapons, causing a pain more intense than the revolting physical reprisals of an Atreus. How curious that, at a time when there existed a society capable of the utmost refinement and civility, a member of that society should produce drama in which savagery reigns — brutality in its most subtle psychological form, but brutality nonetheless. Seneca does occasionally approach the inhumanity of, for example, the Néron-Agrippine clash, as when Atreus succeeds in breaking his brother's spirit and crushing his pride and self-integrity: this aspect of Seneca was quite capable of attracting Racine's attention.

If certain Senecan structures and situations caught Racine's eye, what of the most noticeable feature of the Senecan form — its language and rhetoric? A brief discussion of Racine's might be instrumental in answering the question.

First of all, Racine's education was classical [6] and obviously rhetoric played a great part therein, as Jean Cousin notes: "[La Rhétorique] a formé les auteurs à la composition d'un plan, à la disposition rationnelle d'une claire intrigue, en faisant de l'action de la tragédie une action oratoire, un enchaînement de vrais discours; elle les a formés à l'analyse des sentiments en les obligeant à exposer nettement les liaisons de ces sentiments et leurs nuances...." [7]

---

[6] See B. Munteano, "Port Royal et la Stylistique de la Traduction," *Cahiers de l'Association Internationale des Etudes Françaises*, VIII (juin, 1956), 151-172, and W. Mc. C. Stewart, "L'Education de Racine; le poète et ses maîtres," *CAIEF*, III (juillet, 1953), 55-71.

[7] "Rhétorique latiñe et classicisme français — IV: Rhétorique et tragédie," *Revue des Cours et Conférences*, A. 34, II (1933), 234.

Racine was trained in the logical ordering of phrases and utterances calculated to move the hearer, but under the guise of a completely emotional speech, as in the passion-charged soliloquy of Hermione [8] as the curtain rises on Act V of *Andromaque*, "Où suis-je? Qu'ai-je fait? Que dois-je faire encore? / Quel transport me saisit? Quel chagrin me dévore?" These questions, like those of Oreste in his madness (1629 ff.), are carefully weighed and purposefully ordered to produce the maximum of emotional effect, and thus the irrational quality of Racinian passion is really based upon the systematic logic of rhetoric.

However, rhetorical elements abound in the dramatic works of the century, and are not at all a purely Racinian phenomenon. As Knight has pointed out: "... sur la scène tragique la beauté des discours, une certaine élégance et une certaine rhétorique discrète, appartiennent au genre, non aux personnages." [9]

This tone and this fondness for rhetoric are indeed part and parcel of French Classical theater. But then one should recall that French tragedy was given its impetus in this direction by Seneca, and that it is the Senecan tradition which retains this convention and of which Racine is an heir. Seneca, as pointed out in Part II, brings to French tragedy the fondness for rhetoric and the accompanying elevated tone.

Racine, indeed, utilizes the most noteworthy features of Graeco-Latin rhetoric. Basically they are periphrasis, apostrophe, metonymy, ellipsis, anaphora, enumeration, substitution of abstract for concrete, of plural for singular, the tropes oxymoron and antithesis, and the frequently recurrent figure of interrogation. Leo Spitzer has undertaken a thorough study of Racine's style in his "Die klassische Dämpfung in Racines Stil," [10] in which he points out the effective but discreet use of rhetorical figures, and their part in creating an impersonal tone for the works. The existence of Professor Spitzer's study, plus the very recent

---

[8] The monologue or the *tirade* (when a confidant is present) remains Racine's most skillful device for permitting soul-searching and confession by the protagonist. The lyrical moments in Seneca are expressed in the same fashion, but the emphasis is reversed: the monologue appears more extensively than the protagonist-confidant scene.

[9] *Racine et la Grèce*, p. 350.

[10] *Romanische Stil-und literaturstudien*. I (Marburg, 1931).

contribution of Peter France [11] precludes a similar examination on my part, and therefore I limit my considerations to the salient features.

The principal stylistic device in Racine's first great play, *Andromaque,* and the one which explains why Racine in all his dramatic compositions is clearer and apparently more direct than Seneca, while retaining a rhetorical elegance, is his talent for skilfully employing periphrasis in combination with direct statement. Let us consider the following quotation:

> Mais, Seigneur, cependant s'il épouse Andromaque?
> ... Songez quelle honte pour nous,
> Si d'une Phrygienne il devenoit l'époux! (570-572)

This constitutes a good example of direct statement followed by a circumlocution. The direct manner of speaking is the expression of the character's immediate thought and surprise. The second utterance betrays a certain calculation, an attempt to regain the composure lost. For the goal of most Racinian characters consists not in exposing their true feelings but rather in hiding them. The importance of "le regard" in Racinian tragedy as well as in *La Princèsse de Clèves,* to cite a second example, derives from the seventeenth-century realization that language, ordinarily a vehicle of communication, can be a most effective instrument in impeding communication and concealing one's emotions. Consequently, in the ultra-refined civilization of the second half of the century a gesture, an unguarded glance, a revealing tone of voice may be sufficient betrayal, and very often Racine paints the reaction of the person who has noticed some such action, as in *Britannicus* (1697-1699):

> Burrhus, avez-vous vu quels regards furieux
> Néron en me quittant m'a laissés pour adieux?
> C'en est fait....

Moreover, Racine's perfectly clear language has an unusual kind of transparency: one can understand completely what is

---

[11] *Racine's Rhetoric,* Oxford, 1965.

being said superficially, and yet one also has a good inkling of what is the true nature of those thoughts and intentions of the speaker which he most certainly desires to conceal. An involuntary movement, the rhythm, the tone, or the suitable insertion of a combination of devices, such as periphrasis and direct statement, make this possible.

R. A. Sayce, who has studied this particular combination, writes: "The most obvious use of periphrasis is as euphemism to disguise what is held to be beneath poetic or tragic dignity.... The main purpose [of periphrasis] seems, however, to be narrative. This narrative use is perhaps the principal function of periphrasis in Racine.... It is therefore particularly frequent in the mouths of confidants, who are so often charged with the duty of explaining events to the audience." [12]

In Seneca, periphrasis aids in ornamenting and increasing the volume of a text. Just as in Racine, the expression of ideas of a simple character will often be rendered in periphrasis. For instance, the chorus of Thebans in *Hercules Furens* says (883-887), "Auroram inter et Hesperum, / et qua sol medium tenens / umbras corporibus negat; / quodcumque alluitur solum / longo Tethyos ambitu" ["From the land of dawn to the evening star, and where the sun, holding mid-heaven, gives to shapes no shadows. Whatever land is washed by Tethys' far-reaching circuit..."], when meaning to indicate the world.

Racinian periphrasis usually has an expository function, as it resumes all that background material which had to be excluded because of the conventions of seventeenth-century theater. A second major purpose of periphrasis is to express irony or deceit in a circumlocutory manner. Racine gives a certain fullness, a decorative beauty, and an apparent elevation of the sentiments to his works principally through the adroit use of periphrasis.

However, not all in Racine is expressed indirectly. Direct statement can be used, in moments of great intensity, as effective relief to circumlocution. In contrast to periphrasis, which uses more words than are necessary, direct statement always expresses

---

[12] "Racine's style: Periphrasis and Direct Statement," *The French Mind* (Oxford, 1952), 72.

more than itself. By its very position it gives to the play an intensity which cuts through the elegance of the rhetorical flow of verses: "Je ne t'ai point aimé, cruel? Qu'ai-je donc fait?" (*Andromaque,* 1356). This gives us a clue to a primary difference in the styles of Racine and Seneca.[13] Seneca seldom realizes the value of direct statement outside of its use in stichomythia, and his application of purely periphrastic elements without any compensating precision often creates the impression of bombast. The instances of such effective statements as "Medea superest!" are rare in Seneca.

Any examination of the rhetorical elements of Racine's style would be incomplete without a discussion of metaphor. Because the seventeenth century was interested in action and movement, little attention is paid to the association of forms and colors, but much more to verbs used in a figurative way. A study has been made of these figures for both Corneille and Racine by Roger Crétin in his *Lexique comparé des Métaphores dans le Théâtre de Corneille et de Racine.*[14]

As is the case with Seneca,[15] the metaphors in Racine inspired by nature are relatively few in comparison with those suggested by the human body, with its attitudes, gestures, movements. Both Racine and Seneca viewed the basic material of tragedy as so narrowly concerning man, and indeed those actions which betray the inner man, that their choice of metaphorical elements is comparable from the point of view of the proportion of human to non-human images.

Crétin brings up this important point: "Nous avons dit ailleurs que les images créées de toutes pièces par la sensibilité personnelle de l'écrivain sont rares au XVIIe siècle. Les poètes ne recherchent guère les objets extraordinaires pour les associer d'une manière originale. En matière de métaphores, les clichés existaient alors nombreux et commodes, et la pensée la plus

---

[13] Peter France (*Racine's Rhetoric,* p. 148) concludes, "His [Racine's] use of short sentences in tragedy is one of the most remarkable things about his style and one of those which most distinguishes him from his contemporaries."

[14] Paris: Champion, 1927.

[15] See Howard Vernon Canter's treatise on the *Rhetorical Elements in the Tragedies of Seneca,* Urbana, 1925.

commune se coulait sans effort dans ces moules polis par un long usage." [16]

Indeed many of these metaphors have a history which dates from early French tragedy and its basic model, Seneca. Where Racine says "précipiter dans l'abîme," [17] for example, Seneca has used "dare ad praeceps." This is part of the heritage of the Senecan tradition in French classical theater.

There remains one final point. Having briefly analyzed some aspects of Racine's style, let us now consider it in the light of the "style noble," and especially of Seneca's relation to that style. There undoubtedly exists in French tragedy a style suited to the expression of lofty sentiment, based upon a clear perception of the workings of the human heart and employing verbal devices which best convey these movements. Beginning with Jodelle and his contemporaries, tragedy was composed in a French of a certain elevated level and founded on rhetorical principles. [18] Though the use of rhetoric may be more skilful and subtle by 1660, this level and dignified tone remain basic to the practice of French tragic writing, even for Racine. [19]

In addition to the tone, the same figures of speech occur in Racine and in Seneca and they both indulge in the same general kinds of metaphors. R. A. Sayce has written with reference to the area of periphrasis and direct statement — but which applies to all rhetorical figures in Racine: "... these features are perhaps not confined to Racine,... they may belong to the tragic style in general.... However,... it does seem that not indeed the elements but the modes of combination are his alone." [20]

Certainly school rhetoric may be responsible in part for Racine's demonstrable preference for certain figures. Moreover, Quintilian seems to have been a favorite of Racine [21] and of the

---

[16] *Lexique comparé des Métaphores*, p. V.

[17] See *Mithridate*, 714.

[18] It is interesting to note that *Esther* resembles Renaissance tragedy, particularly sacred tragedy as practiced by a Montchrestien, mainly because of its sententious style.

[19] Cf. France, *op. cit.*, p. 118, n. 5, "Garnier's fine, exaggerated, Senecan rhetoric contains in a crude form all the figures and devices used by Racine."

[20] "Periphrasis," p. 86.

[21] See the copy of the *Institutio Oratoria*, B. N. Fonds Français, 12, 888, annotated by the young Racine.

people at Port-Royal in general.[22] But can one ignore the fact of Seneca's contribution to so many of Racine's predecessors who were refining a genre that Racine himself was to perfect? The works of Garnier, Rotrou, Corneille, to name but three major dramatists, disclose a major debt to Seneca in the domain of expression. It does not seem likely that Racine could follow after these authors without adopting devices which derived, in the first place, from the Roman playwright and which had gradually become part of the form known as *tragédie*.[23]

What this ultimately signifies is that through imitation and utilization Seneca played a role not only in Racine's plots and structures, themes and characters, but indeed even in his own personal means of expression: his style. A stylistic rapport will be then the most pervasive and continuous factor to be found in an examination of the Racinian repertory. And so, even when there may not exist a perceptible trace of Seneca in theme, plot, or character, there will still be present that "style tragique" many of whose components and certainly whose tone ultimately derived from Seneca.

---

[22] See B. Munteano, "La Survie littéraire des Rhéteurs Anciens," *RHL*, 58 (juin, 1958), especially pp. 150-151.
[23] Disappointingly, Mr. France does not choose to commit himself concerning the origin of the rhetorical basis for French tragedy and for Racine's plays in particular (except, indirectly, in the already-cited footnote to p. 118 of his study, where he acknowledges a rapport between Seneca, Garnier, and Racine). Rather, he is content to examine and define those figures which are found in Racine, without regard to their possible sources.

CHAPTER IV

PHÈDRE

In previous chapters we have deliberately isolated particular aspects of the Racine-Seneca relationship (theme, character, structure, and style), the better to analyze and trace each one as it reappeared in the Racinian corpus. *Phèdre,* which stands at the peak of Racine's art as a tragedian, gives us the opportunity to observe all of these factors interacting within a single play.

The years which immediately precede the appearance of *Phèdre* have generally been considered the "Greek" period of Racine: for example, *Iphigénie* includes a great deal of material borrowed from Euripides. But there has been a tendency to overlook the fact of Seneca's continued availability: a French translation of the *Troades* was done by "L. B." in 1674, and Bidar's *Hippolyte,* which probably is indebted to Seneca, was published in 1675. And, of course, Pradon produced his own dramatization of the Phaedra story, *Phèdre et Hippolyte,* almost simultaneously with Racine's version in 1677.

In *Phèdro* Seneca joins forces with Euripides, but as usual Racine does not care to acknowledge Seneca's contribution. Yet the title, in the 1677 edition, was *Phèdre et Hippolyte,* and, before that, *Hippolyte*. It would seem a happy coincidence that the final title chosen by Racine should be precisely that selected by Seneca. Yet the "coincidence" was unavoidable, since both plays turn the spotlight away from Hippolytus, the central character in Euripides, and on that female figure who enters dying in the first act and finally expires in the last, and who in the interim has seen herself responsible for defiling the universe (1633-34),

"Et la mort, à mes yeux dérobant la clarté, / Rend au jour, qu'ils souillaient, toute sa pureté." [1]

In structure, the Racinian play closely resembles the Senecan except in one major aspect: the Hippolyte-Aricie relationship, which does not exist in any of the ancient treatments of the Phèdre story, but is a modern interpolation. [2] There are several scenes in *Phèdre*, however, which, highly important for the plot of the play itself, have a special significance for us in that they are Seneca-inspired. [3]

Moreover, upon proceeding through *Phèdre* one encounters Senecan reminiscences in verse or situation at every major turn of the action: the scene of Phèdre's avowal of love to Hippolyte, Hippolytus' sword being used against him, the recounting of Thésée's captivity (although Racine does not imagine, like Seneca, that Thésée had gone to hell), Hippolyte's death due to Phèdre, part of the *récit de Théramème*, and Phèdre's exoneration of Hippolyte while she is dying.

Verse *rapprochements* will again furnish a concrete basis for a comparative study. The first major instance [4] in which it is very evident that Racine had Seneca in mind occurs in the celebrated scene of Phèdre's declaration of love, Act II, scene 5. Beginning with verse 618 one finds a development which is taken directly from Seneca, and which includes many verses strongly inspired by the Latin text:

---

[1] As I have noted previously, both Racine and Seneca have a genius for creating female characters. Seneca naturally preferred to change the focus of the Euripides' story, and Racine elected to maintain Seneca's alteration in this regard. As a matter of fact, Racine follows Seneca's lead in almost every instance where Seneca deviates from the Euripidean version.

[2] Charles Dédéyan, in his *Racine et sa Phèdre* (Paris, 1965), points out the modern authors that Racine could have used. See especially the chapter, "Les Sources de *Phèdre* et l'Utilisation des Sources," 103-117.

[3] The list includes II, 5, III, 1, III, 5, IV, 2, IV, 6, V, 6, and V, 7. Jean Pommier, on page 193 of his *Aspects de Racine* (Paris, 1954), states that Racine imitates Euripides where Phèdre acts as a wife, and Seneca where she is a widow. This would work out very neatly were it not for IV, 6, and V, 7, where Thésée is alive and Phèdre is still based upon Phaedra of Seneca.

[4] Act I, scene 1 (v. 146), and scene 3 (v. 156, 165-168, 278) possess Senecan traces, but are unimportant.

Madame, il n'est pas temps de vous troubler encore.
Peut-être votre époux voit encore le jour... (618-619)

On ne voit point deux fois le rivage des morts... (623)

J'aime. Ne pense pas qu'au moment que je t'aime.
Innocente à mes yeux, je m'approuve moi-même; ... (673-674)

       ... ces Dieux qui dans mon flanc
Ont allumé le feu fatal à tout mon sang; ... (679-680)

Que dis-je? Cet aveu que je te viens de faire,
Cet aveu si honteux, le crois tu volontaire? (693-694)

Foibles projets d'un cœur trop plein de ce qu'il aime!
Hélas! je ne t'ai pu parler que de toi-même. (697-698) [5]

Besides the quantity of these verses, the significance of them for the needs of characterization is considerable. One should also recall that this is the most dramatic scene of the play, the moment in which Phèdre starts the "machine infernale" of the tragedy.

Phèdre contains other scenes which, though not moments of great intensity, do contribute to the progressive delineation of character. For example, in Act III, scene 1, Phèdre's hope rises as she tells Oenone (783-785):

>Hippolyte, endurci par les sauvages lois,
>Entend parler d'amour pour la première fois.
>Peut-être sa surprise a causé son silence; ...

To which Oenone replies, in a famous verse (789), "Il a pour tout le sexe une haine fatale." After this attempt at dissuasion by the nurse, Phèdre decides to tempt Hippolyte with the throne (803-806):

>Cédons-lui ce pouvoir que je ne puis garder.
>Il instruira mon fils dans l'art de commander.
>Peut-être il voudra bien lui tenir lieu de père.
>Je mets sous son pouvoir et le fils et la mère.

---

[5] Racine 618-622 = Seneca 623-624; R. 623-626 = S. 625-626; R. 673-674, 697-698 = 668-671; R. 693-694 = S. 604-605; R. 705-708 = S. 711-712.

These verses which serve to describe Hippolyte, to show Phèdre entertaining momentary hope, and to reveal how far the queen has gone in her resolution to seduce her stepson are French equivalents of Senecan lines.[6]

An analogous situation comes in the third scene of Act III, where the only verses which smack of Seneca are precisely those five lines in which (1) Oenone first suggests that Phèdre calumniate Hippolyte, and (2) the nurse reveals her character and function in the tragedy (885-889):

> Pourquoi donc lui céder une victoire entière?
> Vous le craignez. Osez l'accuser la première
> Du crime dont il peut vous charger aujourd'hui.
> Qui vous démentira? Tout parle contre lui:
> Son épée en vos mains heureusement laissée, ...[7]

In *Phèdre*, Oenone, like the *Nutrix* in Seneca and in Euripides, insists upon painfully recalling to Phèdre her duties and the blackness of her passion. In addition, both Seneca and Racine maker their *confidentes* conceive of the grounds for accusing Hippolyte, and of the concrete "proof," the sword.

Scene five of the third act contains certain verses whose movement recalls Seneca,[8] but more important here is the situation: that is, the return of Thésée. Racine may have learned from Seneca the dramatic importance of bringing Thésée back in person on stage. Thésée's arrival constitutes the second and decisive *péripétie* of the drama (the first is the false news of his death), and it adds a new dramatic dimension, completely changes the direction of the plot, and casts into an irrevocably immoral state the passion of Phèdre.

The first part of Act IV contains the expression of Thésée's indignation and rage at seeing Hippolyte's sword, the "incriminating" evidence, which has been presented to him by Oenone. The second scene is the focal point, for in it Thésée confronts his son with the charge of hypocrisy and immorality.

---

[6] Racine 783-790 = Seneca 229-243; R. 803-806 = S. 617-622.
[7] These verses copy Seneca's *Phaedra*, 719-724, 729.
[8] 953-958, 975-978 = 850-868 of Seneca.

Hippolytus, in Seneca, is just as unworthy of such an accusation as the Hippolyte of Racine, but for different reasons. Seneca has drawn an unrelenting mysogynist, with little relief to his character. He remains inflexible, and his cries of outrage at the suggestions of the nurse are those of a slapped child, not of a princely young man.

Théramène says to Hippolyte (128), "Avouez-le, tout change!" This typifies the Racinian approach to the characterization of Hippolyte, but it is the exact opposite of what happens in Seneca, where Hippolytus remains a block of stone throughout. Racine has gallicized Hippolytus. To the Senecan qualities of naïveté, inexperience, and innocence, Racine has added the ability to be touched by sentiment, and because this is the first time that Hippolyte has known passion, he is a complete captive. This trait was of course indispensible for a presentation before the French audience of 1677, who would have had little sympathy for a figure of such rigidity and insensitivity as Seneca's Hippolytus.

Act IV, scene 2 opens as Oenone leaves and Hippolyte makes his appearance. (Seneca desires so strongly to concentrate the spectator's attention on the pathology of Phaedra that he does not have a Theseus-Hippolytus confrontation as do Racine and Euripides.) At the sight of Hippolyte, Thésée cries out in anger (1035-1038):

> Ah! le voici. Grands Dieux! à ce noble maintien
> Quel œil ne seroit pas trompé comme le mien?
> Faut-il que sur le front d'un profane adultère
> Brille de la vertu le sacré caractère?

This comes very close to the Senecan version (918-919), "O vita fallax, abditos sensus geris / animisque pulchram turpibus faciem induis" ["O two-faced life, thou keepest thy true thoughts hidden and dost clothe foul purpose with an aspect fair."] [9]

---

[9] In the Mesnard edition, Tome III, p. 364, the editor claims that Seneca here imitated the text of Euripides — which is true. But in the biting *tone* of the French passage Racine more closely approximates Seneca, and I consider the Latin author, therefore, to be the true inspiration for verses 1035-1038 of *Phèdre*.

After Hippolyte's vain effort to justify himself, Thésée calls Neptune to his aid in the famous words of his misdirected curse (1065-1073):

> Et toi, Neptune, et toi, si jadis mon courage
> D'infâmes assassins nettoya ton rivage,
> Souviens-toi que pour prix de mes efforts heureux,
> Tu promis d'exaucer le premier de mes vœux.
> Dans les longues rigueurs d'une prison cruelle
> Je n'ai point imploré ta puissance immortelle.
> Avare du secours que j'attends de tes soins,
> Mes vœux t'ont reservé pour de plus grands besoins:
> Je t'implore aujourd'hui. Venge un malheureux père.

An analysis of Seneca's *Phaedra*, verses 942-954, discloses a similar conception: an appeal to the god of the sea for the accomplishment of a wish which had been granted by Neptune as a reward to the hero; Theseus has reserved the fulfillment of this wish for such a great and unfortunate occasion; even while in prison, Theseus chose not to seek aid from the god — but now he desires it as a means of vengeance (953), "voto perperci: redde nunc pactam fidem" ["I was sparing of this prayer. Keep now thy promised faith."]. Ironically, despite the multiple appeals to the gods in Racine's theater, this instance will be only one of two times that a divinity fulfills a human wish (the other occurring in *Iphigénie*).

The next scene of *Phèdre* keeps the focus on Thésée, as he returns to a more reasonable state of mind, and his paternal affection comes to the fore (1161-1162), "Je t'aimois; et je sens que malgré ton offense / Mes entrailles pour toi se troublent par avance." Conceivably Racine could have had in mind the following lines from *Phaedra* (1114-1116):

> ... O nimium potens,
> quanto parentes sanguinis vinclo tenes,
> natura, quam te colimus inviti quoque.

> [O nature, all too potent, with how strong
> ties of blood dost thou hold parents! how
> we cherish thee even against our wills!]

The following scene, only twenty-six verses in length, comprises the moment of Phèdre's sad awakening to the existence of a rival. There was no Aricie in the ancient conception of the story, and therefore no such scene exists in Seneca. The same may be said of scene five.

The sixth scene reveals Phèdre's self-abhorrence and total despair now that she realizes the existence of a rival. In a moment of magnificent eloquence, she cries out (1269-1278):

> Mes crimes desormais ont comblé la mesure.
> Je respire à la fois l'inceste et l'imposture.
> Mes homicides mains, promptes à me venger,
> Dans le sang innocent brûlent de se plonger.
> Misérable! et je vis? et je soutiens la vue
> De ce sacré soleil dont je suis descendu?
> J'ai pour aïeul le père et le maître des Dieux;
> Le ciel, tout l'univers est plein de mes aïeux.
> Où me cacher? Fuyons dans la nuit infernale.
> Mais que dis-je? Mon père y tient l'urne fatale; ...

Phèdre's panic is understandable: she can flee neither horizontally nor vertically, so to speak — neither to another part of the world nor to the depths of hell. Her relatives are to be found everywhere, accusing her of the "l'inceste et l'imposture." Yet one knows that the most unrelenting critic of Phèdre is Phèdre herself, for she is at the mercy of a truly awful *conscience de soi.* Thus, Phèdre attains the maximum of psychological pain, the point where even death can be of no real assistance. [10]

In the fourth act of *Phédre,* therefore, one encounters many Senecan traits blended into the Racinian play at moments of importance, to express a decisive turn of events, or to emphasize the psychological anguish of a character. Furthermore, in the fifth act Racine continues to demonstrate his respect for Seneca's sense of drama and for his verse also, by including Senecan elements as the basis for the high points.

---

[10] The source of inspiration for most of the passage cited is to be found early in *Phaedra,* at approximately verses 145-158. Racine transfers the portrait of Minos and the underworld from the nurse (in Seneca) to Phèdre, and places it, much more effectively than Seneca, at the moments when Phèdre suffers her agony of despair.

The first five scenes of Act V concern Aricie directly or are based upon insinuations which she imparts to Thésée. As already indicated, this eleminates the possibility of Senecan inspiration. However, the sixth scene, which contains the *récit de Théramène* brings Seneca back into consideration.

The very first line of the *récit* (1498), "A peine nous sortions des portes de Trézène," is a rough paraphrase of the opening remark of the messenger charged with the same sad duty in *Phaedra* (1000), "Ut profugus urbem liquit infesto gradu" ["When with troubled steps he left the city, a fugitive, ..."]. The whole of Théramène's speech contains Senecan reminiscences, especially from verse 1507 through 1550.[11]

Many of the principal details of the two *récits* coincide: the boiling wave that spits out the monster; the creature's bellowing and its general appearance (the head of a bull, scaly, and fire-breathing); Hippolyte's entanglement in the reins and his subsequent death. But here again Racine's mastery becomes evident when one compares his treatment with Seneca's. Racine conveys the plastic quality of the messenger's description, elicits sympathy for the young hero, and pictures the catastrophic effect of Thésée's rash decision, all of this in a very compact passage. He avoids the elegant but superfluous comparisons of the Senecan text (1011-1014):

> Non tantus Auster Sicula diturbat freta
> nec tam furens Ionius exsurgit sinus
> regnante Coro, saxa cum fluctu tremunt
> et cana summum spuma Leucaten ferit.

> ["Not so violently does the south wind distress Sicilia's straits, nor so madly does the Ionian sea swell beneath the north-west's tyranny, when the cliffs tremble under the shock of waves, and the white spray smites Leucate's summit."]

He is also careful to suggest the awful state of Hippolyte's mangled body, whereas Seneca, interested more in forceful expression

---

[11] Cf. Seneca, 1000-1113.

than suggestion, paints the ghastly picture in detail (1093-1104):

> late cruentat arva et inlisum caput
> scopulis resultat; auferunt dumi comas,
> et ora durus pulchra populatur lapis...
>   inde semanimen secant
> virgulta, acutis asperi vepres rubis
> omnisque truncus corporis partem tulit.

["Far and wide the fields are stained with blood, and his head, dashed on the rocks, bounds back from them. The brambles pluck away his hair; the hard stones ravage that lovely face... Thereafter the thickets slash his half-dead body, the rough brambles with their sharp thorns tear him, and every tree-trunk has taken its toll of him."]

Racine's decision not to incorporate certain Senecan elements serves him admirably in two ways. By reducing the messenger's speech (from one hundred and thirteen lines in *Phaedra* to seventy-three in *Phèdre*) Racine is able to create a representation of the play's catastrophe endowed with unusual kinetic qualities; Hippolyte's last few moments of existence seem to pass before us as on a motion picture screen, and they pass quickly, uninterrupted by pointless rhetoric. Secondly, Racine keeps the broad scope in the *récit de Théramène* that he has been at pains to create in all of *Phèdre*, precisely by excising Senecan touches and replacing them with more suitable material. For instance, to demonstrate that the very constitutive elements of nature are repulsed by the monster, Racine has Théramène notice that (1522-1525):

> Le ciel avec horreur voit ce monstre sauvage,
> La terre s'en émeut, l'air en est infecté;
> Le flot qui l'apporta recule épouvanté.
> Tout fuit....

Racine consciously strives to maintain the audience's awareness of the real stage set for *Phèdre:* the universe. Seneca's play does not possess this monumentality of conception, and his choice of detail betrays it.

The *récit* includes references to the "monstre" which slew Hippolyte, and these are just the most concrete allusions to the idea of monstrosity which pervades *Phèdre:* Hippolyte wishes to conquer monsters in imitation of his father; Phèdre's family has been cursed with a monstrous love (and she tells Oenone that she considers the unyielding Hippolyte a "monstre"); finally, Phèdre is conscious that she is a "monstre," an outcast from the human race because of her criminal love. This stylistic device of employing the same key word in prominent places throughout an entire play reappears in Racine's repertory (cf., for example, "sang" in *La Thébaïde*, "les yeux" in *Britannicus*), as it does in Seneca's. In fact John Lapp has discovered the use of the "monster" theme in an analogous way in *Hercules Oetaeus:* "Mais surtout l'ironie de la mort d'Hippolyte rappelle celle d'Hercule, car Hippolyte, 'digne fils d'un héros,' était parti à la recherche de monstres à tuer pour imiter son auguste père. Celui qui cause sa mort est tué, par lui, mais n'en réussit pas moins à le détruire, aidé par un dieu. L'analogie avec la mort d'Hercule est apparente." [12]

Having considered the *récit de Théramène* in its detail as well as in its general structure, we shall, finally, grant that Racine recalled Seneca (among others) [13] when composing the famous passage. But what is significant is Racine's conscious borrowing of material which he then transforms superbly to suit his own artistic ends.

Phèdre's confession, which terminates the play, appears in its outline and in several verses to have been conceived after the Senecan model. In *Phaedra* the heroine enters, confesses the truth while lamenting her loss, then commits suicide. This is

---

[12] "Racine est-il Sénéquien," p. 138.
[13] R. C. Knight (*Racine et la Grèce*, p. 361) has justly concluded: "Le récit de Théramène, enfin, est un amalgame très complexe où, avec les grandes lignes et beaucoup d'expressions empruntées à Euripide et à Sénèque, concourt le souvenir de récits d'Ovide (*Mort d'Hippolyte*, poème), de Quinault (*Bellérophon*), de Gilbert et de Bidar, et jusqu'à une bribe de phrase d'une comédie de Rotrou."

what occurs in *Phèdre,* and, moreover, a part of her explanation seems to have been drawn significantly from the Latin text:

> Non, Thésée, il faut rompre un injuste silence:
> Il faut à votre fils rendre son innocence.... (1617-18)

> C'est moi qui sur ce fils chaste et respectueux
> Osai jeter un œil profane, incestueux.
> Le ciel mit dans mon sein une flamme funeste. (1623-1625)

> ... falsa memoravi et nefas,
> quod ipsa demens pector insano hauseram,
> mentita finxi. vana punisti pater,
> iuvenisque castus crimine incesto iacet,
> pudicus, insons. (1192-1196)

> ["I have lied to you, and the crime which, crazed with passion, I had conceived in my own mad breast, I falsely charged to him. Thou, father, hast punished to no purpose; and the chaste youth, through charge of the unchaste, lies there, all pure and innocent."]

Thus, to the very last scene, reflections of Seneca can be brought to light in Racine's *Phèdre.*

Before considering the heart of Racine's tragedy — the characterization of Phèdre herself — we might profitably take note of another aspect of the play which, like the structure, contributes to its total effect — the style. A brief review of its more prominent traits will suffice.

First of all, one must again insist on the role of rhetoric in Racine. In this, the supreme drama of passion's mastery of the human will, Racine has employed rhetoric to gain emotional effect, and his use of it explains the lucidity of thought and clarity of expression behind emotional outbursts, particularly in the scene of Phèdre's erotic furor (II, 5), "J'aime. Ne pense pas qu'au moment que je t'aime / Innocente à mes yeux, je m'approuve moi-même." Our appreciation of Racine's art is heightened by an awareness of this kind of literary calculation.

This side of his artistic genius may be more fully grasped, if one realizes Racine's deliberate stylistic restraint in *Phèdre,* in which the verses convey a total impression of order and control of form that contrasts marvelously with the desperate and unreasonable nature of the sentiments expressed through the verse.[14] The contrasts which both these devices (rhetoric and restraint) help to create are quite frequent in Racine; antithesis creates tension. The poles of form and content are in perfect balance in Racine precisely because of the interaction due to the clash of opposites.

Racine possessed a talent for organization, not only of the plot, but also of the means of expression, to obtain the maximum effect. *Phèdre,* moreover, is the zenith of Racine's style in the profane dramas. R. A. Sayce remarks: "The features which seem characteristic of him hardly appear in *La Thébaïde* and *Alexandre.* They are most numerous in *Phèdre,* which seems to be the peak of his development (from this point of view)."[15]

Surely another facet of this style which deserves a mention is the role of latinisms in the Racinian vocabulary. Marty-Laveaux, referring to instances where, for example, Racine uses *superbe* in the Latin sense of *fier,* or where he writes *celer* with the Latin meaning of *cacher,* concludes: "Racine a largement contribué à introduire ou à conserver dans la langue française de nombreux latinismes, qui, en même temps qu'ils l'enrichissaient, contribuaient à lui donner cette couleur antique qui sied à la tragédie."[16] *Phèdre,* imbued with so much "couleur antique," contains a significant number of these latinisms.

Given the latinized, rhetorically elegant style that Racine chose as his vehicle for expression, was not Seneca a likely and indeed attractive subject for study, appreciation, and imitation by Racine? Racine found in Seneca an author who had recourse to a great deal of antithesis and periphrasis, whose tone remained singularly lofty and worthy of the tragic genre, whose verse lent itself to imitation and to smooth translation into French. Even these appealing qualities would not be sufficient to add to and enhance the beauty of a Racinian play were it not for Racine's extraordinary good sense and taste in knowing

---

[14] This factor has been profitably analyzed by Leo Spitzer in "Die klassische Dämpfung in Racines Stil." He calls this Racinian technique "Entindividualisierung."

[15] "Periphrasis and Direct Statement," p. 86.

[16] Mesnard edition, Tome VIII, p. x (Preface).

what to select and how to blend it with material of his own. Much as Racine imitated and borrowed from Seneca, the final product is purely Racinian: no "borrowed" verses smack of artificiality precisely because Racine had so absorbed Seneca that to employ Senecan elements must have been almost automatic. Racine's expert training in the classics, including specifically the literary exercises of translating and paraphrasing the ancients, undoubtedly made the recall of an antique source a frequent but natural occurrence. Yet, if there were no connection in tone and style between the two authors, Racine could never have succeeded in introducing so many and differing Senecan elements into his own drama, with such harmonious results.

The *Phèdre* of Racine has several themes in common with Seneca's *Phaedra* which support the central action of the play. As in all of Racine's tragedies there is a question of politics, of the power to govern and the burden it brings. Unlike *La Thébaïde*, however, none of the characters is portrayed as ruthlessly seeking the throne, though Phèdre makes use of the crown as bait in her efforts to ensnare Hippolyte. Indeed, Phèdre clearly offers the political power of the realm to Hippolyte — power which was prized not only by Thésée and Hippolyte (and which had been sought by Phèdre for her sons), but also by Aricie, and, at a former time, her family. Like Madame de La Fayette's character, le Duc de Nemours, Phèdre has learned that the greatest proof of the extent of one's love is the sacrifice of what all others hold dear — a political career.

The theme of responsibility assumes crucial proportions, and is intimately connected with the problems of human liberty, heredity, passion, and the wrath of the gods and fate. These are the basic forces in Phèdre's universe, and her acts are conditioned by them. Let us examine, therefore, the character of Phèdre as she appears in Racine, and what traits she may have in common with Seneca's creation.

Senecan and Racinian characters have a common ground in that their responsibility is evident to the spectator because he has seen them perform the deed. *Phèdre* is the prime example of this, for its fundamental problem is that of personal liberty and responsibility. It is a psychological study of passion with a moral tragedy superimposed upon it. These two aspects are combined within Phèdre: she entertains an illigitimate love, while being fully aware and ashamed of it.

At the play's outset, Phèdre refuses to acknowledge her destiny. She wants to die before dishonoring herself. She is thus not yet *Phèdre*. But once she has yielded to the exciting possibility that Hippolyte may return her passion, she accepts the guilt. Armand Hoog has said, "Il faut le redire, Phèdre n'était pas coupable chez Euripide. En entrant dans le monde de Racine, elle charge le péché sur ses épaules." [17] One should add that the intermediary step between Euripidean and Racinian drama is Seneca's world, where Phaedra appears as definitely accountable. These two then, Phaedra and Phèdre, are supremely conscious of their roles: in spite of themselves they act as forces of evil, responsible for the destruction that threatens the universe.

Moreover, Racine's Phèdre draws upon Seneca's character for a trait, already mentioned, which distinguishes her from the Euripidean conception: her strong sex impulse. Phèdre's genealogy clearly reveals her basic conflict: she is the daughter of Minos (which means *wisdom*) and of Pasiphaé (which signifies *lust*). [18] With this background in mind, one can more fully appreciate the completely sensual meaning which Phèdre attaches to such words as "flamme," "brûle," and "fureur." [19]

Beginning with the very first act, the spectator can perceive the sexual orientation of Phèdre's remarks, too strong to be expressive of that kind of honorable sentiment that characterizes an Antigone or an Hermione (285-288):

> Quand ma bouche imploroit le nom de la Déesse,
> J'adorois *Hippolyte;* et le voyant sans cesse,
> Même au pied des autels que je faisois fumer,

---

[17] "Notre Mère Phèdre," in *Littérature en Silésie* (Paris, 1944), pp. 56-57. The word "péché," however, might leave room for a Jansenist interpretation of *Phèdre* with which I do not agree, and to which I will presently refer.

[18] See Jacques-Gabriel Cahen, *Le Vocabulaire de Racine* (Paris, 1946), p. 138.

[19] I realize that such terms are part of the *précieux* vocabulary to which Racine often has recourse. But in *Phèdre,* as in elsewhere in Racine, these images have a vital and sensual significance that goes beyond the polite gallantry of *préciosité.*

J'offrois tout à ce dieu que je n'osois nommer.
[italics mine]

Moreover, in the famous scene of Phèdre's avowal to Hippolyte, her love is evidently far from platonic. Her declaration, like all such declarations, is an attempt at seduction, and so Racine composes verses which express the physical need to help, to be with, and to posses the loved one (653-662):

> Mais non, dans ce dessein je l'aurois devancée:
> L'amour m'en eût d'abord inspirée la pensée.
> C'est moi, Prince, c'est moi dont l'utile secours
> Vous eût du Labyrinthe enseigné les détours.
> Que de soins m'eût coutés cette tête charmante!
> Un fil n'eût point assez rassuré votre amante.
> Compagne du peril qu'il vous falloit chercher,
> Moi-même devant vous j'aurois voulu marcher
> Et Phèdre au Labyrinthe avec vous descendue
> Se seroit avec vous retrouvée, ou perdue.

Phèdre's desire to possess Hippolyte, and to be the only one in his life, is brought out through the repeated use of pronouns of the first person and other direct references to herself (indeed, verse 656 is the only line without some such reference).

Besides the sensual aspects of Phèdre's love, one must also take note of the directness, indeed brazenness, of her approach ("c'est *moi*, Prince, c'est *moi*") which is surely a trait borrowed from Seneca, in whose play Phaedra rushes on stage in her impatience to see Hippolytus: Phaedra twice falls to her kness, and boldly attempts to embrace him (705), "... etiam in amplexus ruit" ["Even rush into my arms!"].

The device of the sword, taken from Seneca's *Phaedra*, is introduced at this point. It is the tangible evidence that will serve to condemn Hippolyte in Thésée's eyes. Seneca, in fact, has Phaedra use this sword as the means of suicide. Racine, who could not go that far because of the *bienséances,* still dares allow his Phèdre to grasp Hippolyte's blade and thereby to bring out the masochistic element in her sensual love: like Phaedra, she would be thrilled to die at the hands of the loved one.

Once rejected by Hippolyte, Phèdre betrays her sexual frustration. Phèdre, one must remember, can very logically be interpreted as a young woman, sufficiently attractive to entice Hippolyte under other circumstances. This being the case, Phèdre's frustration is all the more intense since she knows that, ordinarily, she would have little difficulty in succeeding with a young man. The unsatisfied passion later expresses itself as resentment when she realizes the impossibility of possessing Hippolyte, because of his attachment to Aricie.

Yet, even after she discovers Hippolyte's sentiments, Phèdre cannot prevent herself from exclaiming, in a cry of sensual despair (1266), "Mon époux est vivant, et moi *je brûle* encore!" Indeed, the same expression characterizes Phèdre's state in her last moments (1637), "J'ai pris, j'ai fait couler dans mes *brûlantes* veines..." [italics added here and in verse 1266 above].

If one keeps this side of Phèdre in mind, one can see that there is a sexual drive behind her actions and perhaps less spiritual torment behind her remorse than has been generally suspected. Moreover, the clairvoyance as to the evil she has produced and the very consciousness of her sad destiny recall the Senecan pattern (of Jocasta, Hecuba, Phaedra and others) rather than, as some have said, the Jansenist one: Phèdre knows that she has been condemned by Venus' hatred, whereas the Jansenist soul is never aware of its precise fate. Because of Phèdre's own admission that she defiled the cosmos, it is very tempting to refer to her as an Eve figure, much as one can view Hercules (of *Hercules Oetaeus*) as a Christ figure. However, the comparison with Eve inevitably smacks of a theological, specifically Jansenist interpretation, which is unnecessary. In fact, a substantial argument against the Jansenist position lies in the very concrete consideration that those verses of *Phèdre* which are most susceptible of such an interpretation are probably no more than the development of a passage of Seneca's *Phaedra*:

> ... ces Dieux qui dans mon flanc
> Ont allumé le feu fatal à tout mon sang. (679-680)

> Et ipsa nostra fata cognosco domus:
> fugienda petimus; sed mei non sum potens. (698-699)

> ["I, too, recognize the fortune of my house: we seek what we should shun; but I am not mistress of myself."]

Racine's Phèdre, however, does differ from Seneca's character in that, despite the force of her lust, she is more sensitive to the immorality of her desires. Seneca's Phaedra revels in her desire, and willfully throws herself at Hippolytus. Phèdre keeps a certain restraint, which causes additional torment: she cannot bring herself to be the shameless creature that Seneca has drawn, and so her frustration is greater. Racine creates a situation where Phèdre descends to the depths of despair, only to see a ray of hope, subsequently blotted out by a new turn for the worse. Euripides also, to be sure, contributes to Phèdre's shame and affliction. R. C. Knight has summarized the contributions in this fashion: "On verra que cette tragédie doit à l'emphatique Sénèque de nombreuses suggestions; ... Plus encore que le bon goût qui a su rejeter tant de fatras, il convient d'admirer le discernement qui a su y démêler quelque traits de génie, et l'art qui, en les adaptant, a fondu ensemble l'héroine éhontée de Sénèque et l'héroine pudique d'Euripide." [20]

The total impression conveyed by Racine's Phèdre, however, is more Senecan than Euripidean, for the daring, sensual side of Seneca's creations was understood by Racine as it never had been by his predecessors. None of the Seneca-inspired writers of regular tragedy from Jodelle through Corneille ever attempted to depict characters tortured by frustrated sexual drives as Seneca had done, or as Racine would do in portraying the sadism of Néron, the lust of Phèdre, or the physical need of Roxane. This significant innovation in French tragedy finds its explanation, in great part, in Racine's admiration for Seneca's finest creations: his passionate, unrestrained characters of considerable magnitude, endowed with tremendous destructive energy.

A technique which serves Racine admirably in the play's best moment, the declaration scene, but which also may be found throughout Racine's repertory, consists in the detailed physical description of a character for the purpose of bringing out the true feelings of that individual, or of the person who describes him. In *Phèdre*, the heroine claims to see Theseus in his son,

---

[20] *Racine et la Grèce*, p. 343. As I have attemped to indicate, however, Phèdre leans more heavily in the direction of the "héroine éhontée" than of the "héroine pudique."

and the ensuing physical portrait of Theseus-Hippolytus (634-644) clearly betrays her passion for her stepson, as does Phaedra in verses 646-662 of Seneca's tragedy.

Miss Elizabeth Evans has made a study of this aspect of Senecan drama, with a view to demonstrating the connection Stoic philosophers established between the "inner" and "outer" man. She observes: "These [Senecan] plays, though based directly on Greek dramas, are by and large more concerned with the use of facial and bodily expression, and the material found here would conform most closely to the third method of studying physiognomy discussed in the Pseudo-Aristotelian handbook, i.e. characteristic facial expressions that are observed to accompany different conditions of mind." [21]

Consequently, Miss Evans traces numerous examples of this device in Seneca, and one can readily conclude that Seneca consciously employed it at moments of tension, with happy result: for example, in the *Troades* Andromacha spies Ulysses and remarks simply but knowingly (522-523), "adest Ulixes, et quidem dubio gradu / vultuque: nectit pector astus callidos" ["Now comes Ulysses, grave and slow of tread; Methinks he plotteth mischief in his heart."].

Racine puts precisely the same technique to good use in his drama, as a means of disclosing the authentic sentiments of a character who would otherwise be capable of concealing them. Néron's "J'entendrai des regards que vous croirez muets" (682) constitutes probably the most refined example of the emphasis Racine's characters place on physical betrayal of emotion. Another noteworthy instance occurs in *Bérénice* where the queen perceives Titus' hesitation (595-596). "Hé bien, Seigneur? Mais quoi? sans me répondre / vous détournez les yeux, et semblez vous confondre." Or again, on a larger scale, the nurse's description of Phèdre's fatal sickness (I, 2) considerably charges the emotional atmosphere, and prepares the spectator for Phèdre's imminent arrival. All in all, therefore, Racine's introduction of such description greatly resembles Seneca's and thus forges another link in the chain of affinity.

---

[21] "A Stoic Aspect of Senecan Drama: Portraiture," *Transactions of the American Philological Association*, LXXXI (1950), 173-174.

However, Racine surpasses Seneca in many cases, for he often turns the final physical position, the last gesture (recounted or seen) of his main figures into a plastic image so that they are caught and immobilized in a typical pose for all time: Oreste and Néron, famous for their seizures of madness, are presented or described in their folly; Bérénice, always the foreigner, the exile in a sense, is caught in the act of leaving Rome and Titus ("Pour la dernière fois, adieu, Seigneur," v. 1506); and, to be sure, Phèdre, who enters in an agony of guilt and self-criticism, and who completes the cycle of the play's action by confessing her guilt, remorse, and self-inflicted death.

Phèdre, endowed with remarkable nobility and lucidity, is therefore a Racinian figure created after careful consideration of the preceding Phèdres who assist in attaining the height of perfection in this portrayal of a soul torn simultaneously by fierce passion and painful introspection.

This conception of character sustains the Racinian tragic sense. For, as it is revealed in its finest example *(Phèdre)*, the tragic view of Racine revolves around the act, consciously committed, for which the character is at least partly responsible.[22] The knowledge of this guilt grows within the character, as does the sentiment which caused the act (passion) until, acutely aware of the hopelessness of success, the heroine attempts to turn the order of the universe into chaos. Just as in Seneca, evil derives from the frustrations and perversions of individual men; it is not an organic part of the universe as Euripides believed.

The self-awareness of a Racinian character would once again distinguish him from his counterpart in Euripides, for example, but not necessarily from the equivalent Senecan figure, for Seneca very often infuses an acute self-consciousness into his creatures. Furthermore, a tragedy which has passion as its tragic motive is bound to be a "tragédie de caractère," in which the hero's downfall

---

[22] Jacques Scherer ("La Liberté du Personnage Racinien," *Le Théâtre Tragique*, Paris, 1962, p. 265) has summarized it well: "Les héros de Racine qui affirment leur responsabilité affirment par là même leur liberté. On ne peut pas être coupable sans avoir pu ne pas l'être. Or, le personnage racinien a souvent un sentiment aigu de sa responsabilité; portant sur lui-même un regard sévère, il se connaît, se juge, et, le cas echéant, se punit. Telle est, de toute évidence, la conduite de Phèdre."

derives from his own personal composition, and thus, unlike the typical Cornelian conqueror, he finds himself unable to sweep aside the obstacles to the satisfaction of his will. Racine and Seneca share this conception in their Phaedra plays: no longer is it man against exterior forces, now it concerns man versus himself: the stoic and the christian conceptions converge at this point.

In this intimate struggle, no other individual can be of assistance. Racine in particular underlines this aspect marvelously by playing upon the irony of family strife: within the most proximate of bonds there grow the seeds of mutual extinction. How significantly at variance are the Cornelian and Racinian points of view on this matter: Corneille sketches the members of a family assaulted by outside pressures; Racine describes the members attacking one another! The lack of charity between characters of the closest relationship increases in Racine's repertory, and there is a consequent movement away from the possibility of love and toward the impossibility of it. Thus the *ilotisme* of Racine's characters seems to be gradually confirmed throughout the evolution of his drama, starting with the basic assumption of the great difficulty of sustaining charitable relationships *(La Thébaïde)* [23] to the impossibility of union in love *(Andromaque* and *Bérénice)*, then to hatred of others (Eriphile in *Iphigénie)*, followed by hatred of self *(Phèdre)*, [24] and finally rejection and loathing of God *(Athalie)*.

This *Weltanschauung*, which betrays a fundamental pessimism, has often been termed "Jansenist" because of its severity. However, although Racine's view may have been sharpened by his training in Jansenist circles, one must also recall that pessimism is typical of the tragic genre, and of Senecan tragedy in particular, so that, again, there is no reason for ascribing it to Jansenism.

Admittedly, the tragic sense in Senecan drama does not approach the profundity of Racine's. There does not appear to

---

[23] Michael Edwards, in *"La Thébaïde" de Racine: clé d'un nouvelle interprétation de son théâtre* (Paris, 1965), p. 17 puts it even more strongly by insisting that the central theme is "le désaccord."

[24] Much in the manner of Pascal's libertine, Phèdre cannot bear what she sees very lucidly to be her own unchangeable nature.

be any evolution of Seneca's tragic conception, and indeed it is not constant from play to play,[25] since a few of his heroes (Hercules, for instance) do succeed in surmounting the obstacles in the fashion of Corneille's individuals.

Moreover, Seneca does not manage the expression of the tragic as well as Racine: the former usually gives free rein to the declaration and catastrophic effects of passion as a stoic lesson on the dangers of excessive sentiment, whereas the latter elects to present the evils of man's self-centeredness within the confines of a restrained form, so that when the emotional explosions occur they are the more striking for their contrast with the orderliness of the structure.

However, Seneca does bring to the theater, for the first time, plots where passion, its effects, and introspection serve to cast society into a disorder, from which most of his characters cannot escape (Andromacha, Hecuba), or whose only relief lies in death[26] (Phaedra). And so, I believe that the hopelessness expressed in many Senecan tragedies constitutes yet another motive for Racine's appreciation of Seneca's plays, for it permitted a literary relationship between *tragedians* to flourish in the most essential area.

---

[25] Norman T. Pratt ("The Stoic Base of Senecan Drama," *Transactions and Proceedings of the American Philological Association*, LXXIX [1948], 1-11) has outlined the two ways in which Seneca conceives of the evil that produces tragedy (p. 3): "The concept which explains much in Seneca may be expressed as follows: in his plays, evil is either externalized as the workings of fate or fortune which can be nullified by reason or endurance, or is thought to be caused by the deterioration of character which results when passion destroys reason."

[26] From a philosophical point of view, suicide is generally unacceptable for a stoic like Seneca. Dramatically speaking, Seneca has rare recourse to suicide, since it offers an all-too-easy exit from the terror of living, source of the tragic pain.

CONCLUSION

The investigation of the extent of the imitation and utilization of an author's works by another is, by nature, a delicate and sometimes dangerous operation: like Procrustes, one runs the risk of shortening or lengthening one's guest to fit a bed. Moreover, Seneca poses an additional problem, for what may seem Senecan at first glance may well derive from Euripides, or may be a commonplace of Latin literature. In my attempt to avoid wholesale impressionism, therefore, I have thought it best to indicate the nature of the Racine-Seneca relationship from the most concrete bases possible: I have usually tried to start the discussion of a particular Racinian play by referring to situations, characters, or verses whose sources lie in the drama of Seneca.

In particular, verse *rapprochements* between Racine's plays and Seneca's can be made quite frequently. They abound especially in *La Thébaïde, Andromaque, Britannicus,* and *Phèdre,* and they support the contention that Racine was influenced by Seneca. Racine's selection and utilization of Senecan verses reveals the touch of the master craftsman. At times, his borrowings serve the needs of characterization, as we saw earlier in the instances of Jocaste and Andromaque. Often, he translates and absorbs into his own drama, almost word for word, short but expressive Senecan passages, such as Theseus' cry in *Phaedra* (1207), "tuque semper, genitor, irae facilis assensor meae," which becomes Thésée's (1572) "Inexorables Dieux, qui m'avez trop servi!" — an excellent way of capturing, in very few words, the catastrophe (Hippolyte's death) in the eyes of Phèdre's spouse.

Or again, Racine will take the central idea of a Seneca text, compress its expression somewhat, and then develop its potential to its utmost by placing it in a different part of the story than it was in Seneca. For example, six verses of *Phèdre* (1273-1278) resume the essential features of sixteen of *Phaedra* (145-158) [1] especially as they translate Phèdre's panic.

In *Britannicus* the least subtle type of connection with the pseudo-Senecan *Octavia* consists in the verse reminiscences. Mesnard has noted a few instances, Herrmann more, and Dreyfus-Brisac [2] even more. Racine does not draw upon the *Octavia* for material for one character alone, but he divides it rather evenly among Britannicus, Agrippine, Burrhus, and Néron, the last figure having a very slight advantage.

The textual borrowings from the pseudo-Senecan play are inserted throughout *Britannicus*, beginning with verse 291 and appearing intermittently through verse 1690, which is but eighty lines from the drama's close. The most striking factor about the verses in question is that they are used in two particular ways: [3] first, in scenes where Néron is engaged in verbal combat; secondly, in those two instances where Agrippine confronts Néron and speaks her mind.

In Act III, scene 1 of *Britannicus*, Burrhus tries vainly to dissuade Néron from his attraction to Junie, and this furnishes us with the longest example of the first possible use of Octavia-inspired material (779-799): [4]

Bur.   ... et satisfait de quelque résistance,
          Vous redoutez un mal foible dans sa naissance....

---

[1] This singular compression of Seneca explains how Racine could have included so much basically Seneca material in *Phèdre* when, by my count, there are only 175 verses of Racine's play which are unquestionable imitations of *Phaedra*.

[2] *Plagiats et Réminiscences ou Le Jardin de Racine*, Paris, 1905.

[3] The exception to this is verse 291, "De mille affreux soldats Junie environnée," spoken by Britannicus. But this verse has a particular reminiscence of the *Octavia* in that it recalls the final scenes of the Latin drama where Octavia is surrounded by Nero's soldiers.

[4] Dreyfus-Brisac *(Plagiats et Réminiscences)* gives these lines as occuring in Act III, scene 2, instead of the correct citation, III, 1. This kind of error is frequent in an otherwise enlightening work.

Si vous daigniez, Seigneur, rappeler la mémoire
Des vertus d'Octavie, indignes de ce prix,
Et de son chaste amour vainqueur de vos mépris;
Surtout si de Junie évitant la présence
Vous condamniez vos yeux à quelques jours d'absence:
Croyez-moi, quelque amour qui semble vous charmer,
On n'aime point, Seigneur, si l'on ne veut aimer.

Néron: Je vous croirai, Burrhus, ...
... lorsque plus tranquille, assis dans le sénat,
Il faudra décider du destin de l'état....
Mais depuis quelques jours tout ce que je désire
Trouve en vous un censeur prêt à me contredire. [5]

This passage resembles in tone, in the Stoic advice of Burrhus, and in several turns of phrase the following segment of *Octavia*, where Nero and Seneca discuss the emperor's moral character (561-579, 588-589):

Sen: vis magna mentis blandus atque animi calor
Amor est....
quem si fovere atque alere desistus, cadit
brevique vires perdit extinctus suas.

Nero: Hanc esse vitae maximam causam reor,
per quam voluptas oritur; ...
Prohibeor unus facere, quod cunctis licet?
Male imperantur, cum regit vulgus duces
Desiste tandem, iam gravis nimium mihi,
instare; Liceat facere quod Seneca improbat.

["This 'Love' is a mighty force of mind, a fond heat of the soul... and if thou cease to feed and foster it, it falls away and quickly is its power dead and lost...
This do I deem the chiefest source of life, whence pleasure hath its birth...
Shall I alone be forbidden what all may do?..."]

The same preoccupations appear in the two passages, and Nero's final menacing words could well have been those of which Racine

---

[5] These last two verses (1095-1096) are inserted here because they too are inspired by the Latin passage, although they occur later in *Britannicus* than the foregoing thirteen verses.

was thinking when he composed the couplet that ends the first quotation.

Before considering the second type of textual *rapprochement* between *Octavia* and *Britannicus*, let us briefly note the last instance where Néron acts like Nero. The effective stichomythia of *Octavia*, verses 447, 450, 453-459, is quite vividly reproduced in the following section of *Britannicus* (1053-1056):

Brit: Ainsi Néron commence à ne se plus forcer.
Néron: Néron de vos discours commence à se lasser.
Brit: Chacun devoit bénir le bonheur de son règne.
Néron: Heureux ou malheureux, il suffit qu'on me craigne.

In *Octavia* Seneca again serves as Nero's interlocutor, but he is attempting to calm the emperor and appeal to his reason. Racine prefers to heighten the tension and permits Britannicus to "play with fire" before the smouldering Néron.

Some of Agrippine's words are echoes of what was said by Agrippina in *Octavia*. The following Racinian quotations, for example, undoubtedly find their source in verses 331-342 and 356-365 of the Latin tragedy in which the chorus repeats the enraged cries of Agrippina, a prisoner aboard a ship caught in a storm. Racine skilfully lays down the Senecan details as the basis for Agrippine's frightening, if somewhat legalistic recounting of her crimes, as well as for what might be called her "historical malediction" — a curse whose consequences will be inscribed in the annals of history.

Vous regnez. Vous savez combien votre naissance
Entre l'empire et vous avoit mis de distance. (1119-1120)
Enfin des légions l'entière obéissance
Ayant de votre empire affermi la puissance,
On vit Claude; et le peuple, étonné de son sort,
Appris en même temps votre règne et sa mort.
   C'est le sincère aveu que je voulois vous faire:
Voilà tous mes forfaits. En voici le salaire. (1191-1196)
Par des fait glorieux tu te vas signaler.
Poursuis. Tu n'as pas fait ce pas pour reculer.
Ta main a commencé par le sang de ton frère;
Je prévois que tes coups viendront jusqu'à ta mère. (1672-1678)
Et ton nom paroîtra, dans la race future,
Aux plus cruels tyrans une cruelle injure. (1691-1692)

CONCLUSION   155

The evident fact that these verses are not consecutive reminds us that Racine does not indulge in word-for-word imitation, but is rather so imbued with a knowledge of Senecan drama that he can, consciously or not, recall several verses to suit a particular need. The above quotations, and also verses 1683 and 1687-1690 of *Britannicus*, [6] emphasize the point that *Octavia*, as regards the Nero-Agrippina clash, forms the historical aftermath of *Britannicus*: it is in the Latin tragedy that one learns of Agrippina's punishment by her son for daring to rival him in ambition. [7]

Through an investigation of textual borrowings one can arrive at an appreciation of Racine's most concrete debt to Seneca. However, indebtedness is not always so specific, but may relate to ideas affecting tone and structure. In the first part of this study an attempt was therefore made to point out the nature and general features of Senecan drama, with an emphasis on its real merits. I indicated the structural concentration characteristic of Seneca, employed particularly, and to an excess, in the Hercules dramas. This investigation proved fruitful when examining *Alexandre* from the same point of view.

This monocentric construction serves to concentrate on the main character, investing him with the quality of introspection so essential to the Stoic depiction of the soul ravaged by emotion and awful self-knowledge. The analysis of this aspect was vital in revealing the affinity between Racine and Seneca in the general conception of character, for the Racinian creations too are very aware of the roles they play and the responsibility for their acts.

To emphasize the torment of the noble tragic character, Seneca composes his works in a grandiose style, quite suited to the expression of intense and lengthy suffering due to adversity. This elevated tone was carried through the Renaissance and early seventeenth-century drama and became an integral part of the

---

[6] Verse 1683 is reminiscent of 619-620 of *Octavia*, and 1687-1690 is similar to *Octavia*, 629-643.

[7] L. Herrmann (*Octavie*, source de *Britannicus*," p. 19) argues convincingly that the image of a rather sympathetic Agrippine is derived, not from Tacitus, but perhaps from *Octavia*, where, while using her son, she retains a certain measure of sympathy for him (Cf. verses 632-645, especially 637).

genre which Racine brought to its moment of perfection: *tragédie*.

But the Renaissance also looked to Seneca for situations (Garnier's *Hippolyte*), themes (suffering and death in Jodelle's *Cléopâtre*), moral content (the guilt of the king in *Saül le Furieux*), and an interpretation of character — an aspect which distinctly ties Jodelle and Garnier to Seneca.

Furthermore, Robert Garnier is the first of three prominent dramatists who will act as points of diffusion for Senecan drama because, in imitating them, younger writers will, consciously or otherwise, be employing Seneca-inspired elements. The other two are Rotrou and Racine.

The 1580-1630 period made use of Seneca in two divergent fashions: as the formal (and moral) model for classical dramaturgy (Brisset's *Agamemnon*); or, as one of the important sources for the violent, often macabre revenge play (Belyard's *Le Guysien*) known as "baroque" tragedy. Significantly, Seneca follows both paths that serious drama takes during these fifty years, and he is thus present when the best elements of both tendencies unite to form *tragédie*.

With Hardy *(Scédase)*, Rotrou *(Hercule Mourant)* and Corneille *(Médée)* one perceives an effort to develop the dramatic aspects of serious plays, while retaining the tone and many of the situations and characters of Seneca. The moral ideas are usually reshaped to fit the standards of succeeding ages (Prevost's *Hercule*).

Racine is the major practitioner of tragedy in the next generation, and from *La Thébaïde* through *Athalie* there exists an affinity of varying degrees between Racine and Seneca, starting with the level of the verse and some of the phraseology as seen in *La Thébaïde*, through the portrayal of Andromaque in imitation of Seneca's Andromacha, to the style, characters, situation and even conception of the tragic that is found in the happiest moment of the Racine-Seneca relationship, *Phèdre*, and finally to the imitation of Seneca's best creation (Medea) in Athalie.

Indeed, Racine borrows heavily from all the aspects of Seneca's drama, except perhaps his specific moral ideas. The Senecan conception is at times pessimistic and tragic and Racine joins him at such moments. But the musings on divine justice and providence contained in the choral odes have no reflection in Racine's profane dramas, for all except poetic justice (as, for example, in Néron's seizure of madness) is banished from Racine's universe by the very nature of his tragic view: the assurance of fair treatment would seriously weaken, if not vitiate, the sentiment of despair which looms large in the delineation of Racine's main figures. Paradoxically, therefore, in his insistence upon the total absence of any ultimate recompense, Racine is more pagan than Seneca.

What particularly strikes the critic examining the Senecan tradition from Jodelle through Racine is that Racine is the only dramatist who knew how to translate and convey the penetration and power of Seneca. Even Corneille does not strike the *sharp* notes which Seneca attains and which Racine re-creates with decisive effect in portraying, for example, the *reconnaissance* of Phèdre as she regards herself and her act with horror — a feeling shared by many Senecan characters. Together Racine and Seneca plumb the depths of their characters' souls with a lucidity and an intensity unknown to other classical tragedians.

Much as Racine was indebted to Seneca, he never chose to acknowledge his indebtedness. The reason for the deliberate concealment of it is not to be discovered in the corpus of Racine's works, although he does refer to Seneca in several prefaces (the last of which is that to *Phèdre*) and in the "Discours prononcé à l'Académie Française à la Réception de MM. de Corneille et de Bergeret" (January 2, 1685). Yet everywhere his approach remains the same: at best, he will indirectly acknowledge that *real* Senecan tragedy has merit (preface to *La Thébaïde*), but usually he will note how he has changed an unhappy Senecan touch (the characterization of Pyrrhus, "Première préface à *Andromaque*," and the shocking accusation against Hippolytus in Seneca, "Vim corpus tulit," which Racine eliminates out of respect for the *bienséances,* as he indicates in the *Préface à Phèdre*). Or again, in the speech of reception for Thomas Corneille, Racine refers to Roman tragedy, but plainly suggests its inferiority: "Personnage [Pierre Corneille] véritablement né pour la gloire de son pays; comparable je ne dis pas à tout ce que l'ancienne Rome a eu d'excellents tragiques, puisqu' elle confesse elle-même qu'en ce genre elle n'a pas été fort heureuse, mais aux Eschyles, aux Sophocles, aux Euripides...."

And yet it is patently clear that Racine did have frequent recourse to Seneca. Why did he prefer to obscure this debt? Perhaps the answer lies, not in Racine's writings, but in the opinions of Seneca which his contemporaries expressed. A sampling of the views on Seneca might therefore be in order here.

Seneca's popularity knew no bounds in the Renaissance and in the early seventeenth century, either among critics or artists; Garnier and Scaliger prominently advocated the Senecan cause. Translations and imitations multiplied through the 1650's, with Malherbe giving his support to this movement by his translations of Senecan prose, and his announced preference for the tragedies of Seneca. Guez de Balzac, in his renowned letter to M. de Scudéry on "La Querelle du Cid," speaks appreciativement of Seneca: "...mais un philosophe dont la dureté n'était pas impénétrable à la joie; duquel il nous reste des satires et des tragédies; qui vivait sous le règne d'un empereur et comédien, au siècle des vers et de la musique." At this same time all of Roman literature enjoyed enormous success in France: Virgil, Tacitus, Horace, Statius, Ovid, *et alii*. Heinsius, a most influential critic, writes and defends a heavily Senecan tragedy, *Herodes*, in 1636. There exists a whole series of letters (1639-1640) between Chapelain and Balzac concerning Seneca: Balzac has been impressed by the writings of the Stoics, and Chapelain desires to learn if Balzac will follow Epictetus, who lived the Stoic life, or Seneca, who did nothing but preach it. Despite this reservation about Seneca's personal morality, Chapelain was, as the editor of his *Lettres* puts it, "grand lecteur et admirateur de Sénèque." [8]

But a divergence of opinion begins to appear in the 1650's, which will intensify during the next three decades. In 1657 l'Abbé d'Aubignac publishes *La Pratique du Théâtre*, in which he roundly criticizes Seneca's lack of dramatic sense while generally approving the efforts of the Greeks. For example: "Mais pour les

---

[8] Jean Chapelain, *Lettres*, ed. Ph. Tamizey de Larroque, 2 vols., Paris, 1880-1883, vol. II, *lettre* XLVIII, n. 5.

CONCLUSION

quatre Grecs qui nous restent, ils ont esté bien plus religieux en la composition du Chœur, que l'Autheur des Tragédies de Seneque; comme ils sçavoient bien mieux que luy l'art et la conduitte de ce genre de Poëme...." [9]

Yet he occasionally grants a word of approval, and he is forced to make this admission: "Et nous voyons que ces Poëmes, qui portent le nom de Senéque, tout irreguliers qu'ils soient, et presque defectueux en toutes leurs parties, passent néantmoins pour excellens au sens de plusieurs par la beauté des discours, par l'energie des expressions, et par la force des sentiments qui s'y lisent." [10]

We must recall that d'Aubignac's adverse attitude towards Seneca comes only two years before Corneille's *Oedipe*, four years before the J.-F. Gronovius edition of the tragedies (*Senecae Tragoediae, cum notis*, Leyden, 1661), generally considered the best text of Seneca's dramas published in the century,[11] and seven years before Racine's introduction of Senecan elements into *La Thébaïde*. And so one cannot conclude that Seneca's popularity had seriously waned, but the critical reactions tend to become markedly hostile.

During the twenty or thirty years following *La Pratique du Théâtre*, several prominent theorists continue the attack on Seneca, generally in favor of Greek art. When referring to Latin drama, Boileau will speak curtly of "la foiblesse latine," [12] or he will expatiate on the subject: "Au reste, il ne faut pas s'imaginer que, dans ce nombre d'écrivains approuvés de tous les siècles, je veuille ici comprendre ces auteurs, à la vérité anciens, mais qui ne se sont acquis qu'une médiocre estime, comme Lycophron, Nonnus, Silius Italicus, l'auteur des tragédies attribuées à Sénèque, et plusieurs autres à qui on peut, non-seulement comparer, mais à qui on peut, à mon avis, justement préférer beaucoup d'écrivains modernes." [13]

---

[9] *La Pratique du Théâtre*, p. 198.
[10] *Ibid.*, p. 284.
[11] Chapelain refers to Gronovius in vol. II, *lettre* LII and *lettre* CCLXXII.
[12] *Œuvres Complètes*, ed. A. Gidel (Paris, 1873), vol. III; *Art Poétique*, chant III, v. 80.
[13] *Ibid.*, vol. II; *Réflexion* VII, pp. 364-365.

Rapin, in his *Réflexions sur la Poétique,* has more than a few words of censure for Roman art, for Seneca in particular (whom he considers pompous and shallow), and for Seneca-inspired Renaissance tragedy. Bouhours, a companion to Rapin and an adviser to Racine and Boileau, deigns to mention Seneca occasionally in *La Manière de bien penser dans les ouvrages de l'esprit,* but he obviously thinks of him not as a dramatist, but as a *déclamateur* who can coin an apt phrase.

Baillet's *Jugemens des Savans,* it seems to me, is little more than a sounding board for the appraisals of a select group, when it comes to matters of literary criticism. The circle of Racine's friends and associates clearly influences the kind of "Jugemens" Baillet includes in his collection. Thus he cites Boileau, Rapin, Bonhours, Père le Bossu, and a few others who dislike Seneca. [14] Even after recognizing the success Seneca had acquired in the seventeenth century, Baillet concludes: "Il semble neanmoins que tous ces éloges ne peuvent nous persuader autre chose, sinon que Sénèque pensoit noblement et parloit bien. Car on peut dire qu'il n'avoit ni la connoissance de l'art Poétique, ni le discernement nécessaire pour le bon usage & la juste application de ses pensées et de ses paroles." [15]

Finally, two critics of the very end of the century echo the same judgement, Fontelle and Saint-Évremond. The former actually appreciates Latin literature except for its tragedy: "Il me paraît encore que, sur la poésie et l'éloquence, les Grecs le cèdent aux Latins. J'en excepte une espèce de poésie, sur laquelle les Latins n'ont rien à opposer aux Grecs; on voit bien que c'est de la tragédie dont je parle." [16] Saint-Évremond's conclusion may

---

[14] In *Jugemens des Savans sur les Principaux Ouvrages des Auteurs* (Paris, 1722-1730, 8 vols.; original date of publication is 1688), Baillet expresses the seventeenth century's general feeling on the question of the authorship of Seneca's tragedies: "*Sénèque* Le Tragique, c'est-à-dire un composé de trois ou quatre Auteurs dont le principal est *Sénèque* le Philosophe." He then proceeds to name *Medea, Hippolytus,* and the *Troades* as authentic compositions of Seneca the philosopher.

[15] *Ibid.,* IV, 168. On pages 167-169 Baillet presents the opinions of "Sénèque le Tragique."

[16] "Digressions sur les Anciens et les Modernes," *Œuvres* (Paris: Salmon, 1825), IV, 245.

be gathered from this short quotation, "Je commencerai par Sénèque, & vous dirai avec la dernière impudence, que j'estime plus sa personne que ses ouvrages." [17]

The verdict would seem to be unanimous, and perhaps it is — if only the critics, most of whom were personally known to Racine, are allowed to speak. If one leaves the realm of theory, the point of view changes radically. Does not Racine himself help to balance the scales, in addition to the other dramatists practicing between 1660 and 1700? [18] Quinault, Boyer, and Dancourt looked to Seneca for *theatrical* elements, not for moralizing sentiments. [19] Pradon, in the prefaces of *Phèdre et Hippolyte* (1677) and *La Troade* (1679), does not share Racine's hesitation in mentioning a debt to Seneca. And the humanist Longepierre seems to boast of his borrowings from Seneca instead of from Corneille, in the preface to *Médée* (1694): "Mais pour me rendre justice, on devoit avoir dit que M. Corneille ayant pris plusieurs pensées dans Sénèque, j'ai cru pouvoir aussi puiser dans la même source, et y en prendre quelques-unes. Voilà la vérité...." [20]

My conclusions are these: first, since Seneca was obviously not repudiated by the practitioners, most of whom were hostile to Racine, it must be that Racine's extreme sensitivity to criticism (cf. his prefaces) prevented him from declaring his obligation to an author whom his circle viewed as "second-rate." The substantiality of his borrowings undoubtedly increased Racine's

---

[17] *Œuvres Melées* (Paris: Barbin, 1690), p. 219.

[18] Besides the tragedians, one should not overlook La Fontaine's fondness for Senecan prose.

[19] Quinault produced *Bellérophon* in 1670; Abbé Claude Boyer's *Agamemnon* (1680) occasionally exhibits a Senecan trace; Dancourt's first (and only?) tragedy, *Hercule* (1683), treats the Hercules story very generally as told by Seneca, with much more and specific indebtedness to the particular structure of Racine's *Andromaque*. Just after the turn of the century, Crébillon *père* takes up the Senecan thread and sews it into his *Atrée et Thyeste* (1707).

[20] Even if Longepierre is on the defensive here (as a reputed humanist and classical scholar he might well want to avoid confessing indebtedness to a modern poet, specifically Corneille), his positive reference to Seneca indicates that he had no qualms about citing the Roman as a reputable source — a citation which is all the more significant for being made by an eminent specialist in *Greek* literature.

reluctance in this matter. Thus, I suspect that the general condemnation of Seneca by Racine's close acquaintances, plus Racine's aversion to disapproval of his own work or its sources (cf. preface to *Mithridate*) made it almost impossible that Seneca should receive the deserved acknowledgment.

Second, Racine's pose at the court was that of the *docte*, whose knowledge extended even to Greek literature in the original language. Given this exalted conception of his own intellectual superiority that Racine endeavored to maintain, it is unlikely that he would have cited an "accessible" author like Seneca when he could just as credibly point to Aeschylus or Sophocles. [21]

However, the influence of Seneca on Racine in particular, and in general on the writers who were creating modern tragedy (Corneille, Shakespeare, Gryphius *et alii*) is both sizable and crucial, and his theater continues to offer moments for inspiration, even for leading contemporary dramatists, as has been revealed in a study of Jean Anouilh's *Médée* and its debt to Seneca. [22]

Clearly, then, an intimate familiarity with Senecan drama furnishes a key to a more profound appreciation of what Racine was endeavoring to accomplish in his own. The exposure of Racine's sensitive and usually unerring choice of Senecan characters, situations, and verse, plus the skill of his compression and insertion of such matter excite increased admiration for the secret of Racine's art: he knew what to appropriate, and what not, and through poetic transmutation and integration of these foreign elements, he makes them his own in a resultant naturalness and simplicity worthy of the highest classical ideals. Thus, the role of Seneca, as of Euripides and others, was to aid Racine in extending the dimensions of his dramatic art, and indeed Racine's unique comprehension and consequent happy transformation of classical authors is undoubtedly a fundamental differentiating factor between a Quinault, a Pradon, and a Racine.

---

[21] For more on Racine the "docte," see Picard, *Carrière*, p. 258.
[22] John C. Lapp., "Anouilh's *Médée:* A Debt to Seneca," *MLN* (March, 1954), 183-187.

SELECT BIBLIOGRAPHY

I. RACINE

ADAM, ANTOINE. *Histoire de la littérature française au XVIIe siècle*, 5 vols. Paris, 1949-1956.
AUERBACH, ERICH. "Racine," *Mimesis*, trans. W. R. Trask, Princeton, 1953, 371-394.
AUBIGNAC, FRANÇOIS HÉDELIN, L'ABBÉ D'. *La Pratique du Théâtre*, ed. P. Martino, 2 vols. Paris, 1927.
BAILLET, ADRIEN. *Jugemens des Savans sur les Principaux Ouvrages des Auteurs*, 8 vols. Paris, 1722-1730.
BÉNICHOU, PAUL. "Racine," *Morales du Grand Siècle*, Paris, 1948, 131-155.
BONNEFON, P. "La Bibliothèque de Racine," *Revue des Cours et Conférences*, V (1898), 169-219.
BORGERHOFF, E. B. O. *Freedom of French Classicism*, Princeton, 1950.
BOILEAU. *Œuvres Complètes*, ed. A. Gidel, Paris, 1873.
BRUNOT, F. *Histoire de la langue française des origines à 1900, Tome IV: la langue classique (1660-1715)*, 2 Parts, Paris, 1939.
BRUNSCHVICG, LÉON. "De l'Ironie dans les Tragédies de Racine," *Revue des Cours et Conférences*, 33 (1931-1932), 1-16. 143-157.
BUSSON, HENRI. *La Religion des Classiques*, Paris, 1948.
CAHEN, J. G. *Le Vocabulaire de Racine*. Paris, 1946.
CHAPELAIN, JEAN. *Lettres*, ed. Ph. Tamizey de Larroque, 2 vols. Paris, 1880-1883.
COUSIN, JEAN. "Rhétorique latine et classicisme français—IV: Rhétorique et tragédie," *RCC*, A. 34, II (1933), 234-243.
CRESSOT, M. "La langue de Phèdre," *Français Moderne*, X (1942), 169-182.
CRÉTIN, ROGER (VERCEL, ROGER). *Lexique comparé des Métaphores dans le Théâtre de Corneille et de Racine*. Paris, 1927.
DANCOURT, FLORENT C. "La Mort d'Hercule," *Le Théâtre à Arras et à Lille en 1683*, ed. Victor Advielle, Paris: Librairie Tresse et Stock, 1893.
DÉDÉYAN, CHARLES. *Racine et sa Phèdre*. Paris, 1965.
DREYFUS-BRISAC, EDMOND. *Phèdre et Hippolyte ou Racine moraliste*. Paris: chez l'auteur, 1903.
———. *Plagiats et Réminiscences ou le Jardin de Racine*. Paris: chez l'auteur, 1905.
EDWARDS, MICHAEL. *"La Thébaïde" de Racine: clé d'une nouvelle interprétation de son théâtre*. Paris, 1965.
FONTENELLE, BERNARD LE BOUVIER DE. *Œuvres*. Paris: Salmon, 1825.

FRANCE, PETER. *Racine's Rhetoric.* Oxford, 1965.
FRANÇOIS, CARLO. "Phèdre et les Dieux," *FR,* XXXV, No. 3 (January, 1962), 269-278.
FRYE, PROSSER, H. "Racine," *Romance and Tragedy,* Boston, 1922, 205-276.
GIRAUDOUX, JEAN. *Racine.* Paris, 1930.
GUTWIRTH, M. "La Problématique de l'innocence dans le théâtre de Racine," *RSH,* 106 (avril-juin 1962), 183-202.
HARTLE, ROBERT. "Racine's Hidden Metaphors," *MLN,* LXXXVI No. 2 (February, 1961), 132-139.
———. "Le Brun's Histoire d'Alexandre and Racine's *Alexandre le Grand,*" *RR,* 48 (1957), 90-103.
HOOG, ARMAND. "Notre Mère Phèdre," *Littérature en Silésie,* Paris, 1944, 21-75.
HUBERT, JUDD. *Essai d'Exégèse Racinienne.* Paris, 1956.
JOVY, ERNEST. *La Bibliothèque de Racine.* Paris, 1933.
KNIGHT, R. C. "A Further Note on Racine's *Thébaïde,*" *French Studies,* X (July, 1956), 254-255.
———. "A Minimal Definition of Seventeenth-Century Tragedy," *FS,* X (October, 1956), 297-308.
———. "Sophocle et Euripide ont-ils 'formé' Racine?" *FS,* V (April, 1951), 126-139.
———. *Racine et la Grèce.* Paris, 1950.
KRUG, A. *Etude sur la Phèdre de Racine et l'Hippolyte de Sénèque.* Colmar, 1862.
LAGA, C. "Didon et Hermione," *Alfa* (publication of the University of Marília, Brasil), No. 2 (Septembro de 1962), 21-42.
LAPP, JOHN. *Aspects of Racinian Tragedy.* Toronto, 1955.
———. "Racine est-il Sénéquien?" *Les Tragédies de Sénèque et le Théâtre de la Renaissance,* Paris: CNRS, 1964, 127-138.
———. "Racine's Symbolism," *Yale French Studies,* IX (1952), 40-45.
MAULNIER, THIERRY. *Racine.* Paris, 1947.
MAURER, KARL. "Racine und die Antike," *Archive für das Studium der neueren Sprachen,* V. 193 (1956-57), 15-32.
MAY, GEORGES. *D'Ovide a Racine.* Paris, 1949.
———. "La Genèse de *Bajazet,*" *Modern Language Quarterly,* IX (June, 1948), 152-164.
———. *Tragédie cornélienne, tragédie racinienne,* Urbana: University of Illinois Press, 1948.
MOORE, W. G. "Le *Bajazet* de Racine: Etude de Genèse," *RSH,* 54 (1949), 69-82.
MORNET, D. *Histoire de la littérature française classique (1660-1700),* Paris, 1940.
MOURGUES, ODETTE DE. *Racine or the Triumph of Relevance.* Cambridge, 1967.
MÜLLER, K. *Die "Phaedra Racines" Quellenstudie über Auseinandersetzung mit. I. birherigen Kritik* (Dissertation), Leipzig, 1913.
MUNTEANO, B. "La Survie littéraire des Rhéteurs Anciens," *RHL,* 58 (juin, 1958), 145-156.
———. "Port-Royal et la Stylistique de la Traduction," *CAIEF,* 8 (juin, 1956), 151-172.

SELECT BIBLIOGRAPHY

NEWTON, WINIFRED. *Le Thème de Phèdre et d'Hippolyte dans la littérature française.* Paris, 1939.
PEYRE, HENRI. *L'Influence des Littératures antiques sur la littérature française moderne.* New Haven, 1941.
PICARD, RAYMOND. *La Carrière de Jean Racine.* Paris, 1956.
POMMIER, JEAN. *Aspects de Racine.* Paris, 1954.
―――. *Créations en Littérature.* Paris, 1955.
POULET, GEORGES. *Études sur le Temps Humain.* Paris, 1949.
RACINE, JEAN. *Œuvres,* ed. Paul Mesnard, *Collection des Grands Écrivains de la France,* 8 vols. Paris: Hachette, 1910-1912.
―――. *Œuvres,* ed. Raymond Picard, *Bibliothèque de la Pléiade,* 2 vols. Paris, 1951.
―――. *Principes de la tragédie,* ed. Eugène Vinaver, Manchester, 1944.
RAPIN, RENÉ. *Reflexions sur l'éloquence, la poétique, l'histoire, et la philosophie.* Paris, 1684.
ROBERT, PIERRE. *La Poétique de Racine.* Paris: Hachette, 1890.
RUDLER, G. "Une source d'*Andromaque*: *Hercule Mourant* de Rotrou," *MLR,* XLL (1917), 286-301, 438-449.
SAINT-ÉVREMOND. *Œuvres Mélées.* Paris: Barbin, 1690.
SAULNIER, V. L. *La littérature française du siècle classique.* Paris, 1943.
SAYCE, R. A. "Racine's Style: Periphrasis and Direct Statement," *The French Mind,* Oxford, 1952, 70-89.
SCHERER, J. *La Dramaturgie Classique.* Paris, 1950.
―――. "La Liberté du Personnage Racinien," *Le Théâtre Tragique,* Paris: CNRS, 1962, 265-269.
SCHLEGEL, A. W. *Comparaison entre la Phèdre de Racine et celle d'Euripide.* Paris: Tourneisen, 1804.
SPITZER, LEO. "Die klassische Dämpfung in Racines Still," *Romanische Stil- und Literaturstudien,* I, Marburg, 1931.
STEGMANN, ANDRÉ. "Les Métamorphoses de Phèdre," *Actes du Premier Congrès International Racinien,* Uzès, 1962, 43-52.
STEWART, WILLIAM. "Le Tragique et le Sacré chez Racine," *Le Théâtre Tragique,* Paris: CNRS, 1962, 271-285.
STEWART, W. McC. "L'éducation de Racine; le poète et ses maitres," *CAIEF,* 3-5 (juillet, 1953), 55-71.
STONE, J. *Sophocles and Racine.* Geneva, 1964.
TOBIN, R. W. "Un Précurseur méconnu de *Phèdre*: *Béral victorieux* de Borée," *RHL,* 65 (jan.-mars, 1965), 103-107.
TRUC, GONZAGUE. "Racine et la Tradition Classique," *Renaissance d'Occident,* VIII (1923), 1130-1140, 1421-1431.
VOLTAIRE, FRANÇOIS MARIE AROUET DE. *Œuvres Complètes,* ed. L. Moland. Paris, 1877.
WEINBERG, BERNARD. *The Art of Jean Racine.* Chicago, 1963.
WHEATLEY, KATHERINE. *Racine and English Classicism.* Austin: University of Texas, 1956.
WHITE, JULIAN, "Racine's *Phèdre*, A 'Sophoclean' and Senecan Tragedy," *Revue de Littérature Comparée,* XXXIX (octobre-décembre, 1965), 605-613.

II. SENECA AND THE SENECAN TRADITION

ALEXANDER, SIR WILLIAM. *The Poetical Works of Sir William Alexander*, ed. Kastner and Charlton, Vol. I. Manchester, 1921. (Introductory essay on the Senecan Tradition.)

AMODIO, ENZO. *Da Euripide a D'Annunzio: Fedra e Ippolito nella Tragedia classica e nella moderna*. Roma: Segati & Ci., 1930.

ANGERS, LE P. JULIEN-EYMARD D'. "Le Renouveau du Stoicisme au XVIe et au XVIIe siècle," *Actes du VIIe Congrès de l'Association Guillaume Budé, 1963*, Paris: Belles Lettres, 1964, 122-153.

———. "Le Renouveau du Stoicisme en France au XVIe et au début du XVIIe siècle [bibliographie]," *Bulletin de l'Association Guillaume Budé*, no. 1 (Mars, 1964), 122-147.

ARNAUD, SIEUR D'. *Agamemnon*. Avignon: Jacques Bramereau, 1642.

BELOE, W. *Anecdotes of Literature and Scarce Books*. London, 1814.

BENOIST, ANTOINE. *Les Theories dramatiques avant les Discours de P. Corneille*. Bordeaux: Annales de la Faculté des Lettres, 1891.

BERANECK, JULES. *Sénèque et Hardy*. Leipzig, 1890.

BIDAR, MATHIEU. *Hippolyte*. Lille: Balthasar Le Francq, 1675.

BILLARD, CLAUDE. *Tragédies Françoises*. Paris: chez Denys Langlois, 1610.

BÖHM, KARL. *Beiträge zur Kenntnis des Einflusses Senecas auf die in der Zeit von 1552 bis 1562 erschienenen Französischen Tragödien*. Leipzig, 1902.

BORÉE, VINCENT. *Les Princes Victorieux*. Lyon: Vincent de Coeursilly, 1627.

BOUHOURS, DOMINIQUE. *La Manière de bien penser dans les ouvrages de l'esprit*. 2e édition. Paris, 1691.

———. *Pensées Ingénieuses des Anciens et des Modernes recueillies par le Père Bouhours*. Paris, 1692.

BOUNIN, GABRIEL. *La Soltane*. Paris: G. Morel, 1561.

BOWERS, F. T. *Elizabethan Revenge Tragedy, 1587-1642*. Princeton, 1940.

BOYER, CLAUDE, ABBÉ (pseudonyme, Pader d'Assézan). *Agamemnon*. Paris: chez Théodore Girard, 1680.

BRAY, RENÉ. *La Formation de la Doctrine Classique en France*. Paris, 1927.

BRISSET, ROLAND. *Le Premier Livre du Théâtre Tragique de Roland Brisset*. Tours: Claude de Montr'œil and Jean Richer, 1589.

CANTER, H. A. *Rhetorical Elements in the Tragedies of Seneca*. Urbana: U. of Illinois Studies, X, 1925.

CATTIN, A. "Le Prologue de la *Phèdre* de Sénèque," *Revue des Etudes Latines*, XXXVIII (1960), 67.

CHANTELOUVE, FRANÇOIS DE. *Tragédie de feu Gaspar de Colligny*. s. l., 1575.

CHARLTON, H. B. *The Senecan Tradition in Renaissance Tragedy*. Manchester, 1946.

CHRESTIEN DES CROIX, NICOLAS. *Rosemonde*. Rouen: Th. Reinsart, 1603.

CORNEILLE, PIERRE. *Théâtre Complet*, ed. Bibliothèque de la Pléiade, 2 vols. Paris, 1950.

COUNSON, A. "L'Influence de Sénèque le Philosophe," *Musée Belge*, VII (1903), 132-167.

CRÉBILLON, P. *Œuvres Dramatiques*. Paris: chez Huet, 1796.

CROISILLE, J. M. "Lieux Communs, *Sententiae* et Intentions Philosophiques dans la *Phèdre* de Sénèque," *REL*, LXII (1964), 276-301.
CUNLIFFE, J. W. *Influence of Seneca on Elizabethan Tragedy*. London, 1893.
DABNEY, LANCASTER. *French Dramatic Literature in the Reign of Henri IV*. Austin, Texas, 1952.
DELCOURT, MARIE. *Etude sur les Traductions des Tragiques Grecs et Latins en France depuis la Renaissance*. Brussels: Hayez, 1925.
DU MONIN, JEAN-EDOUARD. *Orbecc-Oronte*. Paris: Guillaume Bichon, 1585.
ELIOT, T. S. "Seneca in Elizabethan Translation," *Selected Essays*, new edition, New York, 1932, 51-90.
EURIPIDES. *Tragedies*, trans. Arthur M. Way, Loeb Classical Library, London, 1919-1928,
EVANS, ELIZABETH. "A Stoic Aspect of Senecan drama: Portraiture," *Transactions of the American Philological Society*, LXXXI (1950), 169-184.
FAGUET, E. *La Tragédie francaise au XVIe siècle (1550-1600)*. Paris: Fontemoing, 1912.
FLINCK, E. *De Octaviae praetextae auctore*. Helsingfors, 1919.
FORSYTH, ELLIOT. *La Tragédie francaise de Jodelle à Corneille (Le Thème de la Vengeance)*. Paris, 1962.
FRANCQ, H.-G. "Les malheurs d'Oedipe. Etude comparée de l'*Oedipe* de Corneille, Voltaire, Sophocle, Sénèque, Gide, Cocteau," *Revue de l'Université Laval*, XX (1965), 458-480, 560-569, 657-675.
GARNIER, ROBERT. *Œuvres Complètes*, 2 vols. Paris: Garnier Frères, 1923.
GARTON, CHARLES. "The background to Character Portrayal in Seneca," *Classical Philology*, liv (1959), 1-9.
GIANCOTTI, F. *Saggio sulle tragedie di Seneca*. Rome, 1953.
GILBERT, GABRIEL. *Hypolite ou le Garçon Insensible*. Paris: chez Augustin Courbé, 1647.
GRENAILLE, FRANÇOIS DE. *L'Innocent Malheureux ou la Mort de Crispe*. Paris: chez Jean Pasle, 1639.
GRÉVIN, JACQUES. *Théâtre Complet et Poésies Choisies de Jacques Grévin*. Paris, 1922.
GRIFFITHS, R. M. "Les Sentences et le 'but moral' dans les Tragédies de Montchrestien," *RSH*, 105 (janvier-mars, 1962), 5-14.
GRIMAL, PIERRE. "Les Tragédies de Sénèque," *Les Tragédies de Sénèque et le Théâtre de la Renaissance*. Paris: CNRS, 1964, 1-10.
———. "L'Originalité de Sénèque dans la tragédie de *Phèdre*," *REL*, XLI (1963), 297-314.
———. *Sénèque, sa vie, son œuvre*. Paris: Presses Universitaires, 1957.
HANCOCK, JOHN L. *Studies in Stichomythia*. Chicago, 1917.
HARDY, ALEXANDRE. *Théâtre*, ed. E. Stengel, 5 vols. Marburg, 1884.
HENRY, E. and WALKER, B. "Seneca and the *Agamemnon*: Some Thoughts on Tragic Doom," *CP*, LVIII (January, 1963), 1-11.
———. "The Fultility of Action: A Study of Seneca's *Hercules Furens*," *CP*, LX, No. 1 (January, 1965), 11-12.
HERRICK, MARVIN T. *Italian Tragedy in the Renaissance*. Urbana, 1965.
HERRMANN, LÉON. *Le Théâtre de Sénèque*. Paris, 1924.
———. "*Octavie*, source de *Britannicus*," *Bull. Assoc. Guillaume Budé*, avril, 1925, 15-28.
———. *Octavie, tragédie prétexte*, Paris, 1924.

HERRMANN, T. *La Tradition latine dans la tragédie française avant la periode classique.* Copenhagen, 1943.

HORN-MONVAL, M. *Répertoire bibliographique des traductions et adaptations françaises du théâtre étranger du XVᵉ siècle à nos jours,* I et II, Paris, 1958-59.

IAKOB, F. *Die Fabel von Atreus und Thyestes in den wichtigsten Tragödien der Englischen, Französischen und Italienischen Tragödien.* Leipzig, 1907.

JACQUOT, JEAN. "Sénèque, la Renaissance et Nous," *Les Tragédies de Sénèque et le Théâtre de la Renaissance,* Paris: CNRS, 1964, 271-307.

JODELLE, ESTIENNE. *Les Œuvres d'Estienne Jodelle,* ed. Marty-Laveaux, 2 vols. Paris, 1868.

KER, ALAN. "Notes on some passages of the plays of Seneca," *Classical Quarterly,* XII (May, 1962), 48-51.

KERN, EDITH G. *The Influence of Heinsius and Vossius upon French Dramatic Theory.* Baltimore, 1949.

KITTO, H. D. F. *Greek Tragedy: A Literary Study.* New York, 1954.

LANCASTER, H. C. *A History of French Dramatic Literature in the Seventeenth Century,* 9 vols. Baltimore, 1929-1942.

LANSON, GUSTAVE. *Esquisse d'une Histoire de la tragédie française.* Paris, 1954.

LA PINELIERE, GUÉRIN DE. *Hippolyte.* Paris: chez Antoine de Sommaville, 1635.

LAPP, JOHN. "Anouilh's *Médée:* A Debt to Seneca," *MLN,* 69 (March, 1954), 183-187.

LA TAILLE, JEAN DE. *Jean de la Taille und sein Saül le Furieux,* ed. A. Werner. Leipzig, 1908.

LAWTON, H. W. *Handbook of French Renaissance Dramatic Theory,* Manchester, 1949.

LEBEGUE, RAYMOND. "Christianisme et Libertinage chez les Imitateurs de Sénèque en France," *Les Tragédies de Sénèque et le Théâtre de la Renaissance,* Paris: CNRS, 1964, 87-94.

———. *La Tragédie Française de la Renaissance,* 2e edition. Brussels, 1954.

———. *La Tragédie religieuse en France.* Paris, 1929.

———. "La Tragédie shakespearienne en France au temps de Shakespeare," *RCC,* 38 (1937), 385-404, 621-628, 683-695.

———. "Le Théâtre baroque en France," *Bibliothèque d'Humanisme et Renaissance,* II (1942), 161-184.

———. "Tableau de la tragédie française de 1573 à 1610," *Bibliothèque d'Humanisme et Renaissance,* V (1944), 373-393.

LECOUTURIER, N. *Examen de l'Hippolyte d'Euripide, de l'Hippolyte de Sénèque et de la Phèdre de Racine.* Paris, 1818.

L'HÉRITIER DE NOUVELON. *Hercule Furieux.* Paris: Quinet, 1639.

LONGEPIERRE. *Médée.* Paris: chez Delalain, 1786.

LUCAS, F. L. *Seneca and Elizabethan Tragedy.* Cambridge, 1922.

MAINFRAY, PIERRE. *Tragédie des forces incomparables et amours du Grand Hercules.* Troyes: chez Nicolas Oudot, 1616.

MARCOSIGNORI, ANNA MARIA. "Il Concetto di Virtus Tragica nel Teatro di Seneca," *Aevum,* XXIV (1960), 217-233.

MARTI, BERTHE. "Seneca's Tragedies, A New Interpretation," *TAPA*, LXXVI (1945), 216-245.
MATTHIEU, PIERRE. *Clytemnestra*. Lyon: B. Rigaud, 1589.
———. *La Guisade*. Lyon, 1589.
MAURENS, JACQUES. *La tragédie sans tragique: Le néostoïcisme dans l'œuvre de Pierre Corneille*, Paris, 1966.
MOLIERE, J. B. *Œuvres Completes*, ed. Maurice Rat, Bibliothèque de la Pléiade, 2 vols. Paris, 1956.
MONLÉON. *Thyeste*. Paris: chez Pierre Guillemot, 1638.
MONTCHRESTIEN, ANTOINE DE. *Tragédies*, ed. Petit de Julleville. Paris: Librarie Plon, 1891.
MONTREUX, NICOLAS DE (abbé) (pseudonyme, Ollenix du Mont Sacré). *Sophonisbe*. Rouen: chez Raphael du Petit Val, 1601.
MOREL, J. "L'Hercule sur l'Oeta de Sénèque et les Dramaturges Français de l'époque de Louis XIII," *Les Tragédies de Sénèque et le Théâtre de la Renaissance*, Paris: CNRS, 1964, 95-111.
NADAL, OCTAVE. *Le Sentiment de l'Amour dans l'Œuvre de Pierre Corneille*. Paris, 1948.
NISARD, D. *Études des mœurs et de critique sur les poètes latins de la décadence*, vol. I. Paris: Hachette, 1888.
OLDFATHER, PEASE AND CANTER. *Index Vervorum quae in Seneca Fabulae necnon in Octavia Praetexta reperiuntur*, University of Illinois Studies, IV, Urbana, 1918, 1-272.
PARATORE, E. "Originalità del Teatro di Seneca," *Dioniso*, XX, No. 3-4 (Syracuse, 1957), 53-74.
———. "Les Préjugés les plus pernicieux à l'égard de la Littérature Latine," *Bulletin de l'Association Guillaume Budé*, octobre, 1964, 326-341.
PARFAICT (FRERES). *Histoire du Théâtre françois*, 15 Vol. Paris: Morin, 1734-1749.
PATTERSON, WARNER F. *Three Centuries of French Poetic Theory*, 2 vols. Ann Arbor, 1936.
PERRIN, FRANÇOIS. *Sichem Ravisseur*. Rouen: R. du Petit Val, 1606.
PRADON, J. *Les Œuvres de M. Pradon*. Paris: chez Jean Ribou, 1679.
PRATT, NORMAN T., JR. *Dramatic Suspense in Seneca and in his Greek Precursors*. Princeton, 1939.
———. "Major Systems of Figurative Language in Senecan Melodrama," *Transactions and Proceedings of the American Philological Association*, XCIV (1936), 199-234.
———. "The Stoic Base of Senecan Drama," *TAPhA*, LXXIX (1948), 1-11.
———. "Tragedy and Moralism: Euripides and Seneca," in *Phaedra and Hippolytus*, ed. Sanderson and Gopnik, Boston: Houghton Mifflin Company, 1966, 297-307.
PREVOST, JEAN. *Les Tragédies et autres œuvres poétiques de Jean Prevost*. Poitiers: Julian Thoreau, 1613-1614.
QUINAULT, PHILIPPE. *Théâtre*, 3 vols. Paris: Ribon, 1715.
REGNAULT. *Octavie*. Rouen: Jean Petit, 1599.
RIDDLE, LAWRENCE M. *The Genesis and Sources of Pierre Corneille's Tragedies from Médée to Pertharite*, Johns Hopkins Studies, III, Baltimore, 1926.
RIGAL, EUGENE. *Alexandre Hardy et le Théâtre Français a la fin du XVIe siècle et au commencement du XVIIe siècle*. Paris, 1909.

RIGAL, EUGENE. *De Jodelle à Molière.* Paris, 1911.
RIVADEAU, ANDRÉ DE. *Aman.* Poitiers, 1561.
ROBELIN, JEAN. *Thébaïde.* Pont-à-Mousson: Martin Marchant, 1584.
ROTROU, JEAN. *Œuvres,* 5 vols. Paris, 1820.
RUNCHINA, G. *Tecnica drammatica e retorica nella Tragédie di Seneca.* Cagliari, 1960.
SALLEBRAY. *La Troade.* Paris: chez Toussaint Quinet, 1640.
SCHMIDT-WARTENBERG, H. M. *Seneca's Influence on Robert Garnier.* Darmstadt, 1888.
SENECA, L. A. *Ad Lucilium Epistulae Morales,* ed. L. D. Reynolds, 2 vols. Oxford, 1965.
———. *Tragédies,* trans. Léon Herrmann, 2 vols. Paris, 1964.
———. *Seneca's Tragedies,* trans. Frank Justus Miller, Loeb Classical Library, 2 vols. London, 1927.
———. *Tragédies,* trans. Maurice Mignon, 2 vols. Paris: Garnier Frères, 1935.
———. *L. Annaei Senecae, Tragoediae,* ed. Frederick Leo, 2 vols. Berlin, 1879.
———. *Moral Essays,* trans. John Basore, 3 vols. New York: G. P. Putnam's Sons, 1928.
———. *Les Tragédies de Luc. Sénèque, traduites en vers Françoys par Benoist Bauduyn d'Amiens.* Troyes: Noël Moreau, 1629.
SIEGMUND, A. *Zur Textkritik der Tragodie Octavia.* 1907.
SMITH, R. M. *De Arte Rhetorica in L. A. Senecae Tragoediis Perspicua.* Leipzig, 1885.
SPINGARN, JOEL. "Literary Criticism in the Renaissance," Preface to *English Literary Criticism of the 17th Century,* New York, 1905.
STANFORD, W. B. "On some references to Ulysses in French literature from Du Bellay to Fénelon," *Studies in Philology,* L (July, 1953), 446-456.
STEGMANN, A. "La Médée de Corneille," *Les Tragédies de Sénèque et le Théâtre de la Renaissance,* Paris: CNRS, 1964, 113-126.
STUART, DONALD CLIVE. *The Development of Dramatic Art.* New York, 1928.
STUREL, RENÉ. "Essai sur les Traductions du Théâtre Grec en français avant 1550," *RHL,* XX (1913), 269-296.
Théâtre François, ou Recueil des Meilleures Pièces du Théâtre, 12 vols. Paris: La Compagnie des Libraires, s. d.
Tragédie Françoise d'un more cruel, Rouen: A. Cousturier, n. d. (1612-1614?)
WEINBERG, B. *Critical Prefaces of the French Renaissance.* Evanston, 1950.
WIDAL, AUGUSTE. *Etudes sur trois tragedies de Sénèque imitées d'Euripide.* Paris, 1854.
WITHERSPOON, A. M. *The Influence of R. Garnier on Elizabethan Drama.* New Haven, 1924.
WUILLEUMIER, PIERRE. "La Philosophie dans le Théâtre de Sénèque," *Le Théâtre Tragique,* Paris, CNRS, 1962, 265-269.

INDEX OF AUTHORS

Aeschylus (Eschyle), 72, 158, 162
Alberti, Leone Battista, 47
Alexander, William, 20, n. 4, 28, n. 8
Angers, le Père Julien-Eymard d', 11, 49, n. 6
Anouilh, Jean, 162
Aristotle, 29, 47, 48, n. 2
Arnaud Sieur d', 66, n. 33, 72
Aubignac, François Hédelin, abbé d' 158, 159
Auvray, Jean d', 63

Baif, Lazare de, 48, n. 2
Baillet, Adrien, 160
Balzac, Jean-Louis Guez de, 158
Baro, 66, n. 33, 71
Bauduyn, Benoît, 64
Belyard, Simon, 56, 156
Benserade, Isaac de, 69
Beraneck, Jules, 62
Bergeret, 157
Bèze, Théodore de, 48, n. 3
Bidar, Mathieu, 71, 130, 139, n. 13
Billard, Claude, 57-58
Boileau-Despréaux, Nicolas, 53, 159, 160
Borée, Vincent, 63
Borgerhoff, E.B.O., 64, n. 29, 107, n. 23
Bouhours, Dominique, 160
Bounin, Gabriel, 51
Boyer, Claude, 161
Bray, René, 73
Brisset, Roland, 55-56, 156

Cahen, Jacques-Gabriel, 143, n. 18
Canter, H. V., 127, n. 15
Césy, M. de, 105, n. 18

Chantelouve, François de, 52
Chapelain, Jean, 49, n. 6, 158, 159, n. 11
Charlton, H. B., 20, n. 4, 28, 41, n. 8
Chrestien des Croix, Nicolas, 57
Corneille, Pierre, 29, 34, 66-69, 72-76, 79, 85, 102, 118, 119, 127, 129, 146, 149, 150, 156, 157, 159, 161, 162
Corneille, Thomas, 157
Cousin, Jean, 123
Crébillon père, Prosper, 161, n. 19
Crétin, Roger, 127
Croisille, J.-M., 34, n. 3, 41, n. 7

Dancourt, Florent C., 161
Dédéyan, Charles, 12, 131, n. 2
Delaudun d'Aigaliers, Pierre, 56, n. 19
Donatus, 47
Dreyfus-Brisac, Edmond, 152
Du Monin, Jean-Edouard, 52
Durval, Jean-Gilbert, 67
Du Souhait, 56

Edwards, Michael, 149, n. 23
Epictetus, 158
Euripides, 21 ff., 27, 36, 48, n. 2, 54, n. 15, 55, 67, 71, 80, 91, n. 1, 92, 109, 130, 131, n. 1, 133, 134, 139, n. 13, 143, 146, 148, 152, 158, 162
Evans, Elizabeth, 147

Filleul, Nicolas, 51
Fontenelle, Bernard Le Bouvier de, 160
Forsyth, Elliott, 12, 52, 55, n. 18, 67, n. 35

France, Peter, 125, 127, n. 13, 128, n. 19, 129, n. 23.

Garnier, Robert, 47, 52-55, 61, 62, 63, 75, 129, 156, 158
Garton, Charles, 35, n. 4, 43, n. 10
Gilbert, Gabriel, 66, n. 33, 71, 105, 139, n. 13
Giraldi Cinthio, Giambattista, 52
Gombaud, 72, n. 41
Grenaille, François de, 66, n. 33, 71, 105
Grévin, Jacques, 51
Griffiths, Richard, 58, n. 21
Grimal, Pierre, 23, 42
Gronovius, J.-F., 159
Gryphius, 162
Gutwirth, Marcel, 120, n. 5

Hardy, Alexandre, 59-62, 67, 74, 156
Heinsius, Daniel, 63, 79, 158
Herrick, Marvin T., 67, n. 35
Herrmann, Léon, 29, 103, n. 13, 104, 152, 155, n. 7
Hoog, Armand, 143
Horace, 47, 158

Jodelle, Estienne, 47, 48-50, 52, 57, 58, 128, 146, 156, 157
Joyel, 67
Juvenal, 102

Kastner, L. S., 20, n. 4, 28, 41, n. 8
Kern, Edith, 73, n. 42
Knight, R. C., 12, 19, n. 1, 124, 139, 146

La Calprenède, Guillaume de Costes de, 115, n. 2
La Fallette, Marie-Madeleine de, 142
La Fontaine, Jean de, 161, n. 18
Lancaster, H. C., 66, 67, 75, n. 45
Lancelot, Claude, 13
Lanson, Gustave, 47, 48, 54
La Péruse, Jean Bastier de, 48
La Pinelière, Guérin de, 63, 66, 69-70, 76
Lapp, John C., 12, 28, n. 9, 89, 107, 111, n. 28, 139, 162, n. 22
La Taille, Jean de, 51-52
Lebègue, Raymond, 12, 48, n. 3, 54, n. 15, 74, n. 44
Le Bossu, 160

Le Duchat, L.-F., 48, n. 3, 51
Leo, Frederick, 18, n. 3
L'Heritier de Nouvelon, 66, n. 33, 71
Linage, 66, n. 33
Longepierre, 161

Mainfray, Pierre, 59-60, 65
Mairet, Jean, 64
Malherbe, François de, 64, 158
Marolles, 76
Marti, Berthe, 41, n. 7
Marty-Laveaux, Charles, 141
Matthieu, Pierre, 55-56
Maurens, Jacques, 74, n. 43A
May, Georges, 76, n. 47, 105, n. 18, 106
Mesnard, Paul, 152
Miller, Frank Justus, 18, n. 3
Molière, 75
Monléon, 66, n. 33, 70
Montchrestien, Antoine de, 47, 58, 128
Montreux, abbé Nicolas de, 57
Moore, W. G., 105, n. 18, 106
Morel, Jacques, 59, 65, n. 31
Munteano, B., 123, n. 6, 129

Newton, Winifred, 55, n. 17

Ovid, 139, n. 13, 158

Paratore, Ettore, 97, n. 9, 116, n. 3
Pascal, Blaise, 149, n. 24
Patterson, Warner, 47
Percheron, Luc, 56
Perrin, François, 55
Picard, Raymond, 102, 108, 162, n. 21
Plautus, 47
Pollio, M. Vitruvius, 47
Pommier, Jean, 12, 55, n. 17, 131, n. 3
Poulet, Georges, 81, n. 3
Pradon, Jacques, 130, 161, 162
Pratt, Norman T., 17, n. 1, 22, 150, n. 25
Premierfaict, 48, n. 3
Prevost, Jean, 59-60, 156

Quinault, Philippe, 104, n. 17, 106, 139, n. 13, 161, 162
Quintilian, 128

Rapin, René, 160
Regnault, Guillaume, 55-56
Reynolds, L. D., 17, n. 2
Riddle, Lawrence M., 67
Rigal, Eugène, 54, n. 16, 62
Rivaudeau, André de, 51
Robelin, Jean, 52
Robert, Pierre, 103, n. 13
Rotrou, Jean, 63-66, 68, 74, 76, 79, 80, 81, 92, 101, 117, 118, 129, 139, n. 13, 156
Rudler, Gustave, 92, n. 2
Rycaut, Paul, 105, n. 18

Saint-Évremond, Charles de, 160
Sallebray, 66, n. 33, 71-72
Sayce, R. A., 126, 128, 141
Scaliger, Jules-César, 51, n. 8, 63, 158
Scherer, Jacques, 95, 148
Scudéry, Georges de, 158
Sebillet, Thomas, 48, n. 2
Segrais, 105-106
Shakespeare, 162

Sophocles, 48, n. 2, 107, 108, 118, 158, 162
Spitzer, Leo, 124, 141, n. 14
Stanford, W. B., 110
Statius, 82, 158
Stegmann, André, 55, n. 17, 68
Stewart, W. Mc. C., 123, n. 6
Stuart, Donald C., 94

Tacitus, 102, 103, n. 13, 155, n. 7, 158
Terence, 47
Tristan L'Hermite, François, 66, n. 33, 71, 72, 73, n. 41A, 106, n. 20

Vinaver, Eugène, 107
Virgil, 91, 92, 158
Voltaire, François Marie Arouet de, 113
Vossius, 73

Werner, A., 52
Widal, Auguste, 97, n. 9

The Department of Romance Studies Digital Arts and Collaboration Lab at the University of North Carolina at Chapel Hill is proud to support the digitization of the North Carolina Studies in the Romance Languages and Literatures series.

www.ingramcontent.com/pod-product-compliance
Lightning Source LLC
Chambersburg PA
CBHW020416230426
43663CB00007BA/1198